Lose Weight Feel Great

Track Your Success!

ELLINGTON DARDEN, PhD
AUTHOR OF *THE BODY FAT BREAKTHROUGH*

RODALE.

RODALE
wellness

Live happy. Be healthy. Get inspired.

Sign up today to get exclusive access to our authors,
exclusive bonuses, and the most authoritative, useful, and cutting-edge
information on health, wellness, fitness, and living your life to the fullest.

Visit us online at RodaleWellness.com

Join us at RodaleWellness.com/Join

© 2016 by Rodale Inc.

Printed in the United States of America

Rodale Inc. makes every effort to use acid-free ∞, recycled paper ♻.

Book design by Christina Gaugler

ISBN 978-1-62336-743-5

2   4   6   8   10   9   7   5   3   paperback

RODALE.

Follow us @RodaleBooks on

We inspire and enable people to improve their lives and the world around them.
rodalebooks.com

Contents

Lose Weight, Feel Great: The Basics

The Journal

Afterburn

Welcome to Your Weight-Loss Journal

Think of this as your trusty companion to help you track meals, calories, workouts, and your weight-loss success!

Cross your t's and dot your i's, it's time to banish your belly (butt and thighs) for good! Now that you have all the knowledge you need to flatten your belly, it's time to put your brainpower to work. Train your noggin by logging your meals and workouts in this journal. You'll create healthy habits just by paying closer attention to what you eat and how you move. Writing down what you put in your mouth makes you more accountable, and keeps you on track to meet your long-term goals (while also quickly seeing pretty awesome short-term success). And what's more, research shows people who log their meals in a food journal lose up to 6 pounds more than those who don't.

Stick this journal in your purse and you'll never miss a workout or be at a loss for what to eat. Forget your grocery list at home? Turn to page 101 and you'll find a complete list of flat-belly essentials to stock in your kitchen for the week. And when fast food or a restaurant seem to be the only options, just flip to page 113 and scan the selection of healthy on-the-go options. For all the roadblocks, speed bumps, and occasional detours you may encounter over the Flat Belly Breakthrough program, turn your attention to the helpful hints and tips in your journal for extra help.

Flat Belly Breakthrough is your textbook for Weight Loss 101; now here's your core curriculum. Before we get started, commit these six rules to memory.

1. **Prepare balanced meals.**

   Your meal composition should stick to a 50:25:25 rule—that's 50 percent of your plate is carbohydrates, 25 percent is healthy fats, and 25 percent is protein. This 50:25:25 breakdown for each meal influences certain hormones, such as serotonin and cholecystrokinin, which are important in the process of feeling full and satisfied.

2. **Consume smaller meals.**

   Small meals trigger tiny insulin responses throughout the day. Sticking to 300-calorie meals will prevent mood swings, curb cravings, reduce PMS or menopausal tension, eliminate your body's starvation response, aid fat loss because you're not putting your body in storage mode, and keep your energy levels from slumping.

3. **Eat more often.**

   Treat yourself to five or six meals throughout the day (depending on the week in the program). Space each meal to be about 3 hours apart. Breakfast, lunch, and dinner are your pillars, but support them with snacks mid-morning, mid-afternoon, and even one after dinner if you're still hungry.

4. **Track calories per day.**

   When you're trying to lose weight, it's important to keep track of how many calories you eat throughout the day. For fast fat loss your calories should fall between 1,000 and 1,200 calories. Weigh yourself each week to see how your weight fluctuates; sometimes you many need to vary calories week to week in order to find your sweet spot.

5. **Drink more, weigh less.**

   A water bottle is your weapon for weight loss. You will need to drink a gallon of ice water per day on the Flat Belly Breakthrough program. Besides keeping you hydrated and your belly full, water also causes you to get moving—more water means more bathrooms breaks!

6. **Walk daily.**

   Walk at a leisurely pace for 30 minutes within 15 minutes of finishing your evening meal every day.

Your Meal-By-Meal Calorie Breakdown

Tweaking your eating plan is no easy feat—even if you've been following a plan. Luckily, the Flat Belly Breakthrough plan embraces easy-to-find foods that are simple to pull together. Plus, you can welcome back carbohydrates! Just strive for 50:25:25—that's 50 percent carbohydrates, 25 percent fat, and 25 percent protein at each meal. Need a menu? Take a peek at this sample plan for weeks 1 and 2.

Breakfast

1 whole wheat bagel, sliced, with 1 tablespoon light cream cheese

Optional: 1 cup of black coffee

Nutrition: 279 calories, 13.5 g protein, 50 g carbohydrates, 4.3 g fat, 3.5 g saturated fat, 7 g fiber, 413 mg sodium

Lunch

3 ounce ham sandwich made with 2 slices of whole wheat bread, 1 tablespoon of classic mustard, 1 slice of reduced fat Colby-Jack cheese, 2 slices tomato, 2 lettuce leaves

Nutrition: 281 calories, 22 g protein, 31 g carbohydrates, 7.5 g fat, 2.5 g saturated fat, 5 g fiber, 1,101 mg sodium

Mid-Afternoon Snack

$1/_2$ red apple, 3-inch diameter

Nutrition: 58 calories, 0 g protein, 15 g carbohydrates, 0 g fat, 0 g saturated fat, 3 g fiber, 1 mg sodium

Dinner

Three Cheese Ziti Marinara, Michelina's Lean Gourmet

Nutrition: 290 calories, 11 g protein, 48 g carbohydrates, 6 g fat, 2.5 g saturated fat, 4 g fiber, 320 mg sodium

Evening Snack

7 whole, unsalted, organic almonds or cashews

Nutrition: 50 calories, 2 g protein, 2 g carbohydrates, 4 g fat, 0 g saturated fat, 1 g fiber, 0 mg sodium

Master the Inner-Ab Vacuum

Learning the inner-ab vacuum (also referred to as the stomach vacuum) is a simple Flat Belly Breakthrough trick that will do wonders for your waistline. Practicing a 10-second vacuum before you eat will help you handle hunger and know exactly when to stop noshing. But first you need to train your tummy to contract properly. Here's how to start.

- On an empty stomach, lie in bed on your back.

- Place your hands on the bottom of your rib cage, at the top of your abdominals.

- Take a normal breath and forcibly blow out as much air as possible for about 7 or 8 seconds.

- Next, suck in your stomach to the maximum degree using your inner abdominal muscles. You should feel as if you are trying to suck your navel into your backbone. Do not breathe in air during this process; use only your ab muscles.

- Your should feel a concave formation under your rib cage. This concave feel and look is the effect of the stomach vacuum. You will not be able to hold this position very long, probably no longer than 10 seconds.

- Try the vacuum several more times while lying down. If you experience a little light-headedness, that's normal. Rest a bit longer between attempts.

- Now stand and move in front of a mirror to try the vacuum. Because of the forces of gravity, the vacuum is more difficult to do in a standing position. But with a little practice, you'll be able to master it.

- Practice the inner-ab vacuum for 3 consecutive days for about 15 minutes each day.

After about 3 days of training, you should be able to perform the stomach vacuum standing up. Practice it twice before breakfast, lunch, and dinner—or six times a day—for the first 2 weeks. Continue to do the inner-ab vacuum six times a day for the duration of the Flat Belly Breakthrough program, and the involved muscles will become even stronger and more under your control.

How to Guzzle a Gallon of Ice Water Every Day

Because up to 75 percent of your muscle mass is composed of water, there's a variety of reasons that superhydration is the best way to support fat loss. What's more, water is also great for your skin. When fat cells shrink, water rehydrates your skin, leaving it clear, healthy, and resilient to wrinkles!

Still, downing a gallon of ice water in 24 hours may seem intimidating. Fear not, superhydration is easier than you think if you follow these four simple steps:

- Invest in a 32-ounce tumbler—preferably one that is insulated and has a built-in straw.

- You'll need to fill up four times throughout the day to meet your H_2O quota. Keep four hair ties, or rubber bands, on your tumbler. Move them from top to bottom after each refill.

- Pile in the ice cubes—the water you're drinking should be ice cold! Sipping on chilled water makes your metabolism work harder. In fact, some studies indicate drinking 128 ounces (1 gallon) of ice water a day can cause your body's metabolism to burn up to 140 calories to maintain your core temperature.

- Drink most of your water before 5:00 p.m. to avoid midnight runs to the bathroom.

Your Daily Belly-Shrinking Checklist

Good health is made up of everyday choices—and this list will give you a lot of bang for your buck. Choose the easy adjustments that appeal to you most, or try adopting a new one each week. Stick to all these key points and you'll foolproof your diet each day.

Rise and dine.

Eat a breakfast that contains a balance of carbohydrates, fiber, protein, and a little fat. The balance kick-starts your metabolism and fills you up until lunch. Try a slice of whole-wheat toast with natural peanut butter, or a scrambled egg with berries.

Start strong and keep this balance with each dish throughout the day—produce, healthy fats (such as those found in nuts, natural nut butters, avocados, and olive oil), and lean proteins are good foods that will help you feel fuller longer, making you less likely to reach for empty calories between meals.

Swap spices for salt.

Flavor food with herbs, spices, and lemon juice. While sodium can be bad for your heart health, spices have actual health benefits, such as revving up your metabolism (chile pepper) or potentially boosting your immune system (oregano).

THINK BEFORE YOU DRINK

The average person consumes more than 400 calories a day from beverages. Swap out juice and soda for no-cal drinks such as unsweetened tea and water, you could lose up to 40 pounds in a year.

Eat mindfully.

Always eat at the table, chew your food completely, and notice when you're getting full. When you rush to finish your food, you don't pay attention to what or how much you're eating. That means you're more likely to overeat but less likely to enjoy your meals—and what's the fun in that?

Eat well everywhere.

"So many people eat terribly when they go out," says Mary Jane Minkin, MD, a *Prevention* advisory board member. "I'm not saying you can't eat something decadent once in a while—just be sure to check its nutrients online first, if you can, and ask yourself whether it's really worth it." On-the-go without Internet? See page 113 for a list of healthy options at fast-food locations.

Take every opportunity to move.

Stand and pace when you're on the phone; take the long way to the bathroom at work; use stairs instead of escalators. When you look for them, there are dozens of ways to sneak more movement into your day!

Think of exercise as a gift, not a chore.

Many women see exercise as a punishment for "not being fit enough,"—no wonder going to the gym is so discouraging. Ask yourself what extra perks exercise can offer you. Does it relax you? Provide a chance to hang out with friends? Give you a feeling of accomplishment? Make you feel good about how you look or how your body works? Choose the ways to move that are energizing and enhance your daily life.

Reserve your bedroom for sleep and sex.

Make a commitment to ban cell phones, paperwork, and screens of any kind from your bedroom—and turn off all screens in the house an hour before you go to bed. Research shows that the blue light of computers and televisions can mess with natural circadian rhythms as well as levels of melatonin, the sleep hormone.

Make a to-do list at the end of every day.

Write up your list at least an hour before you want to fall asleep. You need to clear your mind by putting on paper all of your concerns for the coming day. Trust that everything will get done when it really needs to get done—tomorrow.

8 Simple Tips for Sticking to the Plan

Crush your hunger and end that gnawing sensation in your stomach with these easy solutions for feeling fuller and more gratified.

1. **Enjoy the spice of life.**

   Top your omelet with hot sauce and splash sriracha on your stir-fry: Though no-frills foods might seem more saintly, flavorful options—especially the spicy variety—are actually more gratifying than bland ones, says Lawrence Cheskin, MD, director of the Weight Management Center at Johns Hopkins Bloomberg School of Public Health.

2. **Have an apple a day.**

   Start your meal with an apple and, research shows, you're apt to eat less overall. The fruit's filling fiber content (a medium one contains up to 5 grams, or roughly a fifth of a woman's daily needs) may be partially to thank. Go with the actual solid fruit: In a study published in the journal *Appetite*, people who sank their teeth into an apple 15 minutes before a pasta meal consumed 15 percent fewer calories than those who had applesauce or apple juice instead.

3. **Learn what full is.**

   You might be full and not realize it. "Most Americans don't even know what satiety feels like, so they keep eating," says Cheskin. Practice aiming for "three-quarters full," says New York City dietitian Lauren Slayton, RD. And remember, the notion that your brain needs time to register fullness is true, says Cheskin: "Take 20 minutes to eat every meal and it'll get easier to know when you should stop."

4. **Stock up on skinny fats.**

   Fat slows the rate at which your stomach and intestines digest food—but when it comes to staving off snack attacks, not all fat is created equal. You might think the fat from a juicy steak would be more substantial than that of an avocado, but it's actually the other way around. A study in the *American Journal of Clinical Nutrition* showed that unsaturated fat—think nuts and vegetable oils—hits the spot better than saturated fat (mostly animal fat, found in meat and dairy).

5. **Ch-Ch-Ch-Chia-fy your foods.**

    Those seeds that make Chia Pets grow could help you shrink. Slayton tells clients to add chia seeds to salads, soups, and smoothies, since they soak up water and swell during digestion.

6. **Multiply and conquer.**

    Instead of a giant sandwich, have half a small one, a side salad, a piece of fruit, and a cup of tea. Or pass up a big bowl of pasta in favor of a piece of seafood, sautéed veggies, and a few whole-wheat noodles on the side. "The meals with multiple lower-calorie elements look like more food, so you're tricking your brain into being satisfied," says Susan Roberts, PhD, a professor of nutrition at Tufts University and creator of MyIDiet.com.

7. **Sip a bit of the bubbly.**

    Carbonation expands the intestinal tract, which makes you feel as if you have a gut full of food. (That's not a license to chug soda; sparkling water, unlike its artificially flavored counterpart, hasn't been tied to weight gain or other issues such as tooth-enamel damage.)

8. **Get a dose of D.**

    When your vitamin D levels are low—and most women's are—it has a negative impact on leptin, the hormone that tells you you've had enough food. (That may explain why studies have linked low D with obesity.) "You can get it from fish like salmon, but it's also smart to supplement with 1,000 IUs of D3 drops like Carlson or Bluebonnet brands," says Slayton.

How to Use Your Journal

Before you get started, take some time to snap a before photo, weigh yourself, and measure your belly, butt, and thighs. You'll be able to enter your Starting Stats on page 23. Your journal provides enough room for you to record your weight, body fat measurements, and even your blood work numbers (with the help of a doctor) as they are right now at the beginning of the program. At the end of each week, your journal will ask you to weigh and measure yourself so you can compare your results from week to week and see the progress you make. Keeping tabs on your metrics will help you see how far you've come and motivate you to meet your goal!

This journal includes logs for 12 weeks so you can cycle through the program twice if you have more weight to lose after the first few weeks, or would like some guidance in your maintenance period. These logs cover food, water, workouts, and walking to help you develop daily routines you can live with even once you've reached your weight-loss goal.

At the beginning of each week, you'll see Your Week at a Glance, which sums up how many strength training workouts you should strive to do and notes when walking workouts should be done. The charts for the first 6 weeks represent just one example of how you can organize your time. One of the strengths of the Flat Belly Breakthrough program is that working out takes up a small percentage of time during the week, so there is some flexibility to how you organize your workouts. Just be sure to leave 72 to 96 hours between each strength routine so your muscles have a chance to repair themselves. Take a 30-minute stroll after dinner each night while sipping your tumbler of ice water. The leisurely pace is easy on your joints, and helps aid digestion before you head to bed.

After Your Week at a Glance and some tips, you will find an overview of your strength routine for the week. You'll be able to track your actual schedule on the exercise and walking logs to see what works best for you. The exercises are described in detail in *Flat Belly Breakthrough*. I have provided recommended reps for each as well as some space to record any notes.

Following the Strength Training Workouts for the week, you will see an After-Dinner Walking Log for the week. While the program simply recom-

USE THE BUDDY SYSTEM

Although you can get terrific results on the Flat Belly Breakthrough program by yourself, you'll probably lose more pounds and inches if you team up with a friend or several friends. Studies suggest that people who exercise together tend to stick with their programs longer and achieve greater results because they motivate each other. Recruit a friend to start the program; shop together, walk together, exercise together and share your challenges and triumphs. My test panelists in Gainesville, Florida, did this and found it inspiring and motivating.

THOUGHT CONTROL

The best way to quell a craving, research shows, is to focus on the positive payoffs of avoiding the food (such as debuting a new bikini) rather than dwelling on the downsides of pigging out. According to study author Sonja Yokum, PhD, practicing the pattern helps make it habit.

mends 30 minutes of walking once a day, you can also try one of the walking workouts in the special Walking tips section that starts on page 189, designed to keep your routine fun and fresh. The Walking Log gives you space to record the date, what type of activities you did, and the duration of your walk in the space below.

The Sleep Log comes next and provides a place to note your weekly sleep patterns. We ask you to note the time you go to sleep, wake up, the quality of sleep achieved, and any additional notes on your sleep time. It is critical to get $8^{1}/_{2}$ hours of sleep each night, plus, if possible, a 30-minute nap each afternoon. Extra sleep and rest are important because more than 50 percent of fat loss occurs during sleep, and 99 percent of muscle building takes place at night. We also provide you sleep tips underneath these logs to make sure you get adequate rest every night.

Next, you'll find enough food log pages for 7 days. The *Flat Belly Breakthrough* book introduces simple meal plans and options that will help you stay on track for maximum weight loss by learning the importance of portion control and superhydration—that is, drinking a gallon of ice water every day. But, in case you're traveling without the book on hand, we've squeezed an abridged version of healthy meals, grocery lists, on-the-go options, and tips for drinking a gallon of ice water into a special Grocery Guide, which starts on page 97.

Finally, each week will end with a weekly measurements sheet. Here you can measure your weight, body fat percentage, and circumference of your belly, butt, and thighs to keep track of how many inches and pounds you're losing. All you need are a bathroom scale, measuring tape, and your thumb and index finger. You'll also have room to record any observations or additional notes. If you are also tracking your blood pressure, blood glucose, or other metrics, remember to make an appointment with your doctor every 12 weeks or so.

You can make routines easier or harder simply by adding a few reps or changing weights, and you can move workouts around to better fit your schedule. Whatever you do, tracking it in this journal can help you see what's working for you (or not) and will make it even easier to turn up your fat burn and lose weight!

On the next few pages, you'll see sample journal pages filled out—you don't have to do it exactly like this, though. Ultimately, this journal is your weight-loss tool, so use it however works best for you!

Sample Weekly Measurements Log

Taking weight and circumference measurements weekly is useful because it lets you know what is happening in specific areas of your body. For the most accurate weight measurement, remove clothing and shoes and weigh yourself in the morning. Be sure to use the same scale when weighing yourself each week. Use a plastic tape measure to determine the following and record your numbers.

THE PINCH TEST

You can get a fair estimate of your percentage of body fat without calipers by doing the pinch test. It requires taking two measurements: one on the back of the upper arm and the second beside the navel. Record the measurements in the chart on page 17 and using the skin-fold thickness chart to estimate body fat percentage.

- Locate the back of the arm (triceps area) midway between the shoulder and elbow. Let the arm hang loosely at your side.

- Grasp a vertical fold of skin between your right thumb and first finger. Pull the skin and fat away from your arm. Make sure the fold includes just skin and fat and no muscle.

- Measure with a ruler the thickness of the skin to the nearest quarter of an inch. (It may be easier to enlist a friend.) Be sure to measure the distance between the thumb and the finger. (Do not press the ruler against the skin, which may flatten the skin.)

- Take two separate measurements of the triceps skin-fold thickness, releasing the skin between each measure. Record the average of the two.

- Locate the second skin-fold site, which is immediately adjacent to the right side of the navel.

- Grasp a vertical fold of skin between the thumb and first finger and follow the same measuring technique as described above.

- Take two separate measurements of the abdominal skin-fold thickness and record the average of the two.

- Add the average triceps skin-fold measurement to the average abdominal skin-fold measurement. This is your combined total.

PINCH TEST MEASUREMENTS

	BEFORE	AFTER
Right triceps		
Right abdominal		
Total		
Body fat percent		
Fat pounds		

ESTIMATED PERCENTAGE OF BODY FAT

SKIN-FOLD THICKNESS	PERCENT FAT	PERCENT FAT
TRICEPS PLUS ABDOMINAL	MEN	WOMEN
¾ inch	5–9	8–13
1 inch	9-13	13–18
1¼ inches	13–18	18–23
1½ inches	18–22	23–28
1¾ inches	22–27	28–33
2¼ inches	27–32	33–38
2¾ inches	32–37	38–43

MEASUREMENTS

DATE: *January 2*

Body Weight: *157.6*

Body Fat Percentage: *31.2%*

MEASUREMENTS

Waist: *29.625"*
(2" above navel)

Waist: *32"*
(at navel)

Waist: *33.5"*
(2" below navel)

Hips: *40.75"*
(largest protrusion)

Left Thigh: *24.25"*
(just below the buttocks crease)

Right Thigh: *24'*
(just below the buttocks crease)

Left Upper Arm: *6.75"*
(hanging in middle)

Right Upper Arm: *6.375"*
(hanging in middle)

ADDITIONAL NOTES: _____

_____

_____

_____

_____

_____

_____

_____

_____

_____

_____

_____

FOOD LOG

	FOOD	TIME	CALORIES	NOTES
Breakfast (300 calories)	2 eggs, scrambled 1½ sliced whole wheat toast w/ pat butter black tea	7:30 a.m.	265	felt full
Lunch (300 calories)	turkey sandwich w/ cheese apple water	1:00 p.m.	220	
Snack (50 calories)	yogurt	3:00 p.m.	50	
Dinner (300 calories)	Healthy Choice Chicken Alfredo w/ Broccoli unsweetened iced tea wedge of cheese	6:30 p.m.	310	LOVE this frozen dinner!
Snack (50 calories)	cashews	8:00 p.m.	50	

WATER LOG: ⊗   1 Gallon or four 32-ounce tumblers

Strength Training Workouts

Do 1$\frac{1}{2}$ slow reps of each move below in 15-second, 15-second, 15-second, negative-accentuated style, followed immediately by the number of regular-speed reps indicated in the chart.

MOVE	WORKOUT 1	WORKOUT 2
	DAY/DATE: *January 4*	DAY/DATE: *January 7*
Forward Crunch	Reps: 8	Reps: 9
Oblique Crunch (right and left)	R: Reps: 8 L: Reps: 8	R: Reps: 9 L: Reps: 9
V-Crunch	Reps: 8	Reps: 9
Pushup	Reps: 8	Reps: 9
Body Weight Squat	Reps: 8	Reps: 9

After-Dinner Walking Log

M: *30 mins* TU: *20*   W: *30*   TH: *30*   F: *30*   SA: *40*   SU: *35*

Sleep Log and the Importance of Snoozing

Sleep is one of the most powerful, yet underutilized, tools for weight loss. In fact, a recent study reported that people who logged 8$\frac{1}{2}$ hours of rest per night lost significantly more body fat than those who dozed for only 5$\frac{1}{2}$ hours.

What's more, in the study the sleep-deprived group also dropped up to 60 percent more muscle than the group who slept more. Those 3 hours of missing sleep caused a shift in metabolism that made the body want to store fat at the expense of lean muscle.

Log your snoozes to see how sleep affects your appetite, weight loss, and energy levels each day. Here's a sample log and a few tips to get you started.

DAY	BEDTIME	WAKING TIME	SLEEP QUALITY	NOTES
Monday	11:00 p.m.	6:00 a.m.	poor	tossed and turned need to go to bed by 10
Tuesday	10:00 p.m.	6:00 a.m.	good	
Wednesday	10:00 p.m.	6:30 a.m.	restful	woke up refreshed
Thursday	10:00 p.m.	6:45 a.m.	very good	
Friday	11:30 p.m.	9:00 a.m.	eh	dinner party went late too much wine!
Saturday	11:00 p.m.	7:00 a.m.	ok	
Sunday	11:30 p.m.	6:45 a.m.	poor	stayed up too late watching TV

BETTER THAN SHEEP:
6 Ways to Sleep More Soundly

Quit tossing and turning. These tricks will help you wake up feeling rested and ready for the day!

- Set a bedtime, and stick to it.
- Ditch the afternoon coffee run.
- Avoid alcohol, too.
- Take a warm shower, or bath, before bed.
- Flip your TV off before dozing off—even the tiniest bit of light from a screen can cause restlessness.
- Create a cave. Keeping your bedroom cool and quiet helps your body temperature naturally prep for sleep.

Starting Stats

Nothing motivates you like seeing change happen before your eyes! Use this space to record your starting point of overall health before you begin the Flat Belly Breakthrough program. There will be checkpoints to help you stay on track along the way, and you can compare them to these starting points to see how far you've come after just 2 weeks, or after 6, or even 12!

Your Before Photos

Wear a solid-color bathing suit or bikini. Stand against an uncluttered, light-colored background. Have the person with the camera stand where he or she can see your entire body in the viewfinder. Stand relaxed for three pictures: front, right side, and back. Don't suck in your stomach. Retake these photos in 6 weeks so you can compare.

DATE:_____

Body Weight:_____   Body Fat Percentage:_____

MEASUREMENTS

Waist:_____
(2" above navel)

Left Thigh:_____
(just below the buttocks crease)

Waist:_____
(at navel)

Right Thigh:_____
(just below the buttocks crease)

Waist:_____
(2" below navel)

Left Upper Arm:_____
(hanging in middle)

Hips:_____
(largest protrusion)

Right Upper Arm:_____
(hanging in middle)

ADDITIONAL NOTES: _____

_____

_____

_____

_____

_____

_____

_____

_____

_____

_____

_____

_____

YOUR WEEK AT A GLANCE

DAY	WORKOUT	MINUTES
1	Strength Training Workout 1 + After-Dinner Walk	20 + 30
2	After-Dinner Walk	30
3	After-Dinner Walk	30
4	Strength Training Workout 2 + After-Dinner Walk	20 + 30
5	After-Dinner Walk	30
6	After-Dinner Walk	30
7	After-Dinner Walk	30

What You'll Do This Week

EXERCISE

Day 1: Perform the 15-15-15 style, followed by 8 regular reps of each exercise.

Day 4: Perform the 15-15-15 style, followed by 9 regular reps of each exercise.

NUTRITION

Adjust your calorie intake to 1,000 calories per day.

Belly Toning Tip

SAY ADIOS TO SORENESS! A study in the *International Journal of Sports Nutrition and Exercise Metabolism* found that vitamin C may reduce exercise-induced muscle soreness. Researchers found those who took the vitamin had less muscle pain for the first 24 hours than the others, probably because C helps reduce inflammation. Until researchers determine the best dose, keep soreness at bay by eating plenty of foods rich in vitamin C, such as bell peppers and citrus fruits.

EXCUSE-PROOF YOUR WEEK

Dieting doesn't have to rule your life. Seek these weekly hints when your new routine heads toward bumpy roads.

Lose Weight, Not Friends

Ever notice that the day you announce you're starting a new diet, your friends go AWOL? Here's why: Cutting calories causes your level of serotonin (a feel-good brain chemical) to nosedive, leaving you cranky and unpleasant to be around.

To keep your serotonin levels in check, figure out how many calories your body needs based on your activity level (find the formulas at WomensHealthMag.com/weight-loss/calculate-your-calories). And make sure those calories are split evenly among protein, whole grains, and produce at every meal.

"Unbalanced meals—made entirely of refined carbs, for example—cause blood-sugar fluctuations that make you irritable," says Caroline M. Apovian, MD, director of the Nutrition and Weight Management Center at Boston Medical Center.

Apovian also recommends adding omega-3 fatty acids to your diet, because research shows that they may fight depression and slow digestion, which helps you stay full longer. (Try eating two or three 3-ounce servings of salmon a week, or adding a tablespoon of olive oil, canola oil, or flaxseeds into your daily meals.)

EXERCISE LOG

Strength Training Workouts

Do $1^1/_2$ slow reps of each move below in 15-second, 15-second, 15-second negative-accentuated style, followed immediately by the number of regular-speed reps indicated in the chart.

MOVE	WORKOUT 1	WORKOUT 2
	DAY/DATE:	DAY/DATE:
Forward Crunch	Reps: 8	Reps: 9
Oblique Crunch (right and left)	R: Reps: 8 L: Reps: 8	R: Reps: 9 L: Reps: 9
V-Crunch	Reps: 8	Reps: 9
Pushup	Reps: 8	Reps: 9
Body Weight Squat	Reps: 8	Reps: 9

After-Dinner Walking Log

M:_____ TU:_____ W:_____ TH:_____ F:_____ SA: _____ SU:_____

SLEEP LOG

DATE:_____

DAY	BEDTIME	WAKING TIME	SLEEP QUALITY	NOTES
Monday				
Tuesday				
Wednesday				
Thursday				
Friday				
Saturday				
Sunday				

SLEEP WREAKER: *Sleeping In*

No alarm clock, no stressful commute, and often, no morning meal—leading to a gorgefest around noon. "If you don't eat until lunch, you'll be starving and think you can eat the equivalent of two meals," says Susan Bowerman RD, assistant director of the UCLA Center for Human Nutrition. "Breakfast tends to be the lowest-calorie meal of the day, so skipping 300 calories and tacking on an extra 600 later certainly isn't going to help you drop pounds."

Damage control: No matter what time you crawl out of bed, chow down! "Eating helps rev your metabolism, which starts your calorie burn," says Bowerman. When you do, throw back some coffee, too. Caffeine is a central nervous system stimulant, so a cup of joe can increase your calorie burn and torch more than 100 calories a day. (Not a java fan? Brewed decaffeinated tea also works.) Then finish your brunch on a sweet note: Researchers from Tel Aviv University recently found that chasing a big breakfast with a small dessert—yes, dessert!—may even help dieters lose more weight and keep it off, possibly by lowering levels of the hunger hormone ghrelin, which may help ward off future cravings.

FOOD LOG

DATE:_____

	FOOD	TIME	CALORIES	NOTES
Breakfast *(300 calories)*				
Lunch *(300 calories)*				
Snack *(50 calories)*				
Dinner *(300 calories)*				
Snack *(50 calories)*				

WATER LOG: ○ ○ ○ ○   1 Gallon or four 32-ounce tumblers

FOOD LOG

DATE:_____

	FOOD	TIME	CALORIES	NOTES
Breakfast *(300 calories)*				
Lunch *(300 calories)*				
Snack *(50 calories)*				
Dinner *(300 calories)*				
Snack *(50 calories)*				

WATER LOG:　○　○　○　○　　1 Gallon or four 32-ounce tumblers

FOOD LOG

DATE:_____

	FOOD	TIME	CALORIES	NOTES
Breakfast *(300 calories)*				
Lunch *(300 calories)*				
Snack *(50 calories)*				
Dinner *(300 calories)*				
Snack *(50 calories)*				

WATER LOG: ◯ ◯ ◯ ◯   1 Gallon or four 32-ounce tumblers

FOOD LOG

DATE:_____

	FOOD	TIME	CALORIES	NOTES
Breakfast *(300 calories)*				
Lunch *(300 calories)*				
Snack *(50 calories)*				
Dinner *(300 calories)*				
Snack *(50 calories)*				

WATER LOG: ○   ○   ○   ○   1 Gallon or four 32-ounce tumblers

FOOD LOG

DATE:_____

	FOOD	TIME	CALORIES	NOTES
Breakfast *(300 calories)*				
Lunch *(300 calories)*				
Snack *(50 calories)*				
Dinner *(300 calories)*				
Snack *(50 calories)*				

WATER LOG: ◯ ◯ ◯ ◯   1 Gallon or four 32-ounce tumblers

FOOD LOG

DATE:_____

	FOOD	TIME	CALORIES	NOTES
Breakfast *(300 calories)*				
Lunch *(300 calories)*				
Snack *(50 calories)*				
Dinner *(300 calories)*				
Snack *(50 calories)*				

WATER LOG: ◯ ◯ ◯ ◯   1 Gallon or four 32-ounce tumblers

FOOD LOG

DATE:_____

	FOOD	TIME	CALORIES	NOTES
Breakfast *(300 calories)*				
Lunch *(300 calories)*				
Snack *(50 calories)*				
Dinner *(300 calories)*				
Snack *(50 calories)*				

WATER LOG: ○ ○ ○ ○   1 Gallon or four 32-ounce tumblers

MEASUREMENTS

DATE:_____

Body Weight:_____   Body Fat Percentage:_____

MEASUREMENTS

Waist:_____
(2" above navel)

Waist:_____
(at navel)

Waist:_____
(2" below navel)

Hips:_____
(largest protrusion)

Left Thigh:_____
(just below the buttocks crease)

Right Thigh:_____
(just below the buttocks crease)

Left Upper Arm:_____
(hanging in middle)

Right Upper Arm:_____
(hanging in middle)

ADDITIONAL NOTES: _____

_____

_____

_____

_____

_____

_____

_____

_____

_____

_____

_____

_____

YOUR WEEK AT A GLANCE

DAY	WORKOUT	MINUTES
1	Strength Training Workout 1 + After-Dinner Walk	20 + 30
2	After-Dinner Walk	30
3	After-Dinner Walk	30
4	Strength Training Workout 2 + After-Dinner Walk	20 + 30
5	After-Dinner Walk	30
6	After-Dinner Walk	30
7	After-Dinner Walk	30

What You'll Do This Week

EXERCISE

Day 1: Perform the 15-15-15 style, followed by 10 regular reps of each exercise.

Day 4: Perform the 15-15-15 style, followed by 11 regular reps of each exercise.

NUTRITION

See how your body is adapting to reduced calories, but don't dip below 1,000 calories per day!

Belly Toning Tip

YOUR BRAIN ON BREAKFAST A recent study that used brain scans to investigate breakfast's effect on eating later in the day was presented at the Neuroscience 2012 conference. Subjects who skipped breakfast were more attracted to images of high-calorie grub—and consumed 20 percent more calories, on average, at lunch—than those who ate in the a.m. The culprit? The orbitofrontal cortex, a part of the brain that processes the reward value of tastes and smells.

EXCUSE-PROOF YOUR WEEK

Dieting doesn't have to rule your life. Seek these weekly hints when your new routine heads toward bumpy roads.

Lose Weight, Not Your Mind

So much of weight loss is focused on what you'll look and feel like when you reach your goal weight. It's time to change that. "To maintain motivation for any behavioral change, the key factor is to identify a concrete reason for doing it that is grounded in today, in feeling better and being more successful at what you do every day," says Michelle Segar, PhD, behavior-change expert at the University of Michigan and author of *No Sweat: How the Simple Science of Motivation Can Bring You a Lifetime of Fitness*. So swap your focus on the future for thinking about how eating well and working out will keep you feeling amazing in the present.

To do that, Dr. Segar recommends sussing out what she calls a "goal clout" for each healthy habit: Identify a reason for sticking to the behavior, and make sure it's relevant to your daily life. Emphasize the positive, like the endorphin rush you get after a workout, rather than negative, like beating yourself up for wanting a bite of cake. Between concentrating on the present and mixing things up with miniature goals that have nothing to do with weight, you'll keep both your body and brain in tip-top shape.

Strength Training Workouts

Do $1^1/_2$ slow reps of each move below in 15-second, 15-second, 15-second negative-accentuated style, followed immediately by the number of regular-speed reps indicated in the chart.

MOVE	WORKOUT 1	WORKOUT 2
	DAY/DATE:	DAY/DATE:
Forward Crunch	Reps: 10	Reps: 11
Oblique Crunch (right and left)	**R:** Reps: 10 **L:** Reps: 10	**R:** Reps: 11 **L:** Reps: 11
V-Crunch	Reps: 10	Reps: 11
Pushup	Reps: 10	Reps: 11
Body Weight Squat	Reps: 10	Reps: 11

After-Dinner Walking Log

M:_____ TU:_____ W:_____ TH:_____ F:_____ SA: _____ SU:_____

SLEEP LOG

DATE:_____

DAY	BEDTIME	WAKING TIME	SLEEP QUALITY	NOTES
Monday				
Tuesday				
Wednesday				
Thursday				
Friday				
Saturday				
Sunday				

Log More Z's

We know, we know—if you could lose a pound every time you heard about the advantages of sleep, you'd never have to work out again. But if 7 to 9 hours of shut-eye still isn't a priority, here's some incentive. Not only does deep sleep kick up production of tissue-repairing growth hormone, studies show that lack of it is a weight-gain double whammy: It prompts your body to consume more calories and shuts down its ability to recognize a full stomach. When you're tired, your gut produces more ghrelin, a chemical that triggers sugar cravings. "It causes your body to seek quick energy from food to try to keep you awake," says neurologist Chris Winter, MD, medical director of the Martha Jefferson Hospital Sleep Medicine Center in Charlottesville, Virginia. Meanwhile, fatigue suppresses leptin, a fat-cell hormone that tells your brain, "OK, stop eating now." For this reason, says Winter, "prioritizing sleep is probably the best thing you can do, recovery-wise, to meet your body-shaping goals."

Sneak in More Shut-Eye: Set an alarm for an hour before bed, then power down. Not only are electronics distracting, but the specific light they emit can affect your sleep quality.

FOOD LOG

DATE:_____

	FOOD	TIME	CALORIES	NOTES
Breakfast *(300 calories)*				
Lunch *(300 calories)*				
Snack *(50 calories)*				
Dinner *(300 calories)*				
Snack *(50 calories)*				

WATER LOG: ◯ ◯ ◯ ◯   1 Gallon or four 32-ounce tumblers

FOOD LOG

	FOOD	TIME	CALORIES	NOTES
Breakfast *(300 calories)*				
Lunch *(300 calories)*				
Snack *(50 calories)*				
Dinner *(300 calories)*				
Snack *(50 calories)*				

WATER LOG: ◯ ◯ ◯ ◯   1 Gallon or four 32-ounce tumblers

FOOD LOG

DATE:_____

	FOOD	TIME	CALORIES	NOTES
Breakfast (300 calories)				
Lunch (300 calories)				
Snack (50 calories)				
Dinner (300 calories)				
Snack (50 calories)				

WATER LOG: ◯ ◯ ◯ ◯   1 Gallon or four 32-ounce tumblers

FOOD LOG

DATE:_____

	FOOD	TIME	CALORIES	NOTES
Breakfast *(300 calories)*				
Lunch *(300 calories)*				
Snack *(50 calories)*				
Dinner *(300 calories)*				
Snack *(50 calories)*				

WATER LOG: ◯ ◯ ◯ ◯   1 Gallon or four 32-ounce tumblers

FOOD LOG

DATE:_____

	FOOD	TIME	CALORIES	NOTES
Breakfast *(300 calories)*				
Lunch *(300 calories)*				
Snack *(50 calories)*				
Dinner *(300 calories)*				
Snack *(50 calories)*				

WATER LOG: ◯ ◯ ◯ ◯   1 Gallon or four 32-ounce tumblers

FOOD LOG

DATE:_____

	FOOD	TIME	CALORIES	NOTES
Breakfast *(300 calories)*				
Lunch *(300 calories)*				
Snack *(50 calories)*				
Dinner *(300 calories)*				
Snack *(50 calories)*				

WATER LOG: ◯ ◯ ◯ ◯   1 Gallon or four 32-ounce tumblers

FOOD LOG

DATE:_____

	FOOD	TIME	CALORIES	NOTES
Breakfast *(300 calories)*				
Lunch *(300 calories)*				
Snack *(50 calories)*				
Dinner *(300 calories)*				
Snack *(50 calories)*				

WATER LOG: ◯ ◯ ◯ ◯   1 Gallon or four 32-ounce tumblers

MEASUREMENTS

DATE:_____

Body Weight:_____   Body Fat Percentage:_____

MEASUREMENTS

Waist:_____
(2" above navel)

Waist:_____
(at navel)

Waist:_____
(2" below navel)

Hips:_____
(largest protrusion)

Left Thigh:_____
(just below the buttocks crease)

Right Thigh:_____
(just below the buttocks crease)

Left Upper Arm:_____
(hanging in middle)

Right Upper Arm:_____
(hanging in middle)

ADDITIONAL NOTES: _____

_____

_____

_____

_____

_____

_____

_____

_____

_____

_____

_____

_____

YOUR WEEK AT A GLANCE

DAY	WORKOUT	MINUTES
1	Strength Training Workout 1 + After-Dinner Walk	20 + 30
2	After-Dinner Walk	30
3	After-Dinner Walk	30
4	Strength Training Workout 2 + After-Dinner Walk	20 + 30
5	After-Dinner Walk	30
6	After-Dinner Walk	30
7	After-Dinner Walk	30

What You'll Do This Week

EXERCISE

Day 1: You'll be adding a new move, a dumbbell curl, to your workouts this week. Perform the 15-15-15 style, followed by 12 regular reps of each exercise.

Day 4: Increase the weight of your dumbbells 5 percent, perform the 15-15-15 style, followed by 8 regular reps of each exercise.

NUTRITION

Weigh yourself at least three times a week. While a variation of 1 to 2 pounds is normal, an increase of 4 to 5 pounds is a sign it's time to tweak your calories.

Belly Toning Tip

BOOST YOUR WATER INTAKE The benefits: Dehydration substantially slows your metabolic rate—so even if you're killing it at the gym, you could be negating the calorie-burning advantages if you aren't drinking enough H_2O, says Shawn Talbott, PhD, a nutrition biochemist in Salt Lake City. And it's not just the eight-glasses-a-day (or 64 ounces) rule you've heard time and time again. Experts advise downing an additional 16 to 20 ounces of water for every hour you train.

EXCUSE-PROOF YOUR WEEK

Many of the Flat Belly Breakthrough test panels saw incredible results in just 2 weeks. Keep your momentum going from Week 1 with this quick tip.

Lose Weight, Not Time

In a recent study, 41 percent of women cited "not enough time" as the reason they don't eat better. Spending just an hour or two on the weekend shopping for a week's worth of healthy meals and getting a jumpstart on the prep work (cutting veggies, making marinades) will save you time and pounds in the long run. A survey by the CDC found that almost 40 percent of people who lost a significant amount of weight and kept it off planned their weekly meals.

"When you don't map out your meals, you're too tempted to grab whatever's nearby, which is often high-calorie junk," says Elizabeth Ricanati, MD, founding medical director of the Lifestyle 180 program at the Cleveland Clinic.

Need help planning? Flip to page 97 for the Lose Weight, Feel Great Grocery Guide.

If swigging the recommended amount of water feels like a Herculean task in itself, remember that most standard bottles of water contain 16 ounces, so four of them (not eight) equal eight glasses. And on the Flat Belly Breakthrough program you'll want to double your intake! Make sure you're checking off each glass in your daily water log.

DATE:_____

Strength Training Workout

Do $1\frac{1}{2}$ slow reps of each move below in 15-second, 15-second, 15-second negative-accentuated style, followed immediately by the number of regular-speed reps indicated in the chart. For workout 2, increase the weight of dumbbells by 5 percent.

MOVE	WORKOUT 1	WORKOUT 2
	DAY/DATE:	DAY/DATE:
Forward Crunch	Reps: 12	Reps: 8
Oblique Crunch (right and left)	R: Reps: 12 L: Reps: 12	R: Reps: 8 L: Reps: 8
V-Crunch	Reps: 12	Reps: 8
Pushup	Reps: 12	Reps: 8
Body Weight Squat	Reps: 12	Reps: 8
Dumbbell Curl	Reps: 12	Reps: 8

After-Dinner Walking Log

M:_____ TU:_____ W:_____ TH:_____ F:_____ SA: _____ SU:_____

SLEEP LOG

DATE:_____

DAY	BEDTIME	WAKING TIME	SLEEP QUALITY	NOTES
Monday				
Tuesday				
Wednesday				
Thursday				
Friday				
Saturday				
Sunday				

5 Must-Haves to Wake-Proof Your Bedroom

- Room-darking shades or blackout curtains: Cuts the light and noise levels and even saves on thermal energy loss
- Hypoallergenic comforter: Stay itch- and sneeze-free with cool, easy-to-clean fabrics
- Sleep mask or eyeshade: Keeps the light out even when the window is open
- Perfect pillow: Pick a pillow to match back, side, or stomach sleeping style. Always check neck and spine alignment for proper fit.
- High thread-count sheets: Seek the higher thread count for the most luxurious feel. Look for pima or Egyptian cotton.

FOOD LOG

DATE:_____

	FOOD	TIME	CALORIES	NOTES
Breakfast (300 calories)				
Snack (50 calories)				
Lunch (300 calories)				
Snack (150 calories)				
Dinner (300 calories)				
Snack (100 calories)				

WATER LOG: ◯ ◯ ◯ ◯   1 Gallon or four 32-ounce tumblers

FOOD LOG

DATE:_____

	FOOD	TIME	CALORIES	NOTES
Breakfast *(300 calories)*				
Snack *(50 calories)*				
Lunch *(300 calories)*				
Snack *(150 calories)*				
Dinner *(300 calories)*				
Snack *(100 calories)*				

WATER LOG: ◯ ◯ ◯ ◯   1 Gallon or four 32-ounce tumblers

FOOD LOG

DATE:_____

	FOOD	TIME	CALORIES	NOTES
Breakfast (300 calories)				
Snack (50 calories)				
Lunch (300 calories)				
Snack (150 calories)				
Dinner (300 calories)				
Snack (100 calories)				

WATER LOG: ◯ ◯ ◯ ◯   1 Gallon or four 32-ounce tumblers

FOOD LOG

DATE:_____

	FOOD	TIME	CALORIES	NOTES
Breakfast (300 calories)				
Snack (50 calories)				
Lunch (300 calories)				
Snack (150 calories)				
Dinner (300 calories)				
Snack (100 calories)				

WATER LOG: ◯ ◯ ◯ ◯   1 Gallon or four 32-ounce tumblers

FOOD LOG

DATE:_____

	FOOD	TIME	CALORIES	NOTES
Breakfast (300 calories)				
Snack (50 calories)				
Lunch (300 calories)				
Snack (150 calories)				
Dinner (300 calories)				
Snack (100 calories)				

WATER LOG: ◯ ◯ ◯ ◯   1 Gallon or four 32-ounce tumblers

FOOD LOG

DATE:_____

	FOOD	TIME	CALORIES	NOTES
Breakfast *(300 calories)*				
Snack *(50 calories)*				
Lunch *(300 calories)*				
Snack *(150 calories)*				
Dinner *(300 calories)*				
Snack *(100 calories)*				

WATER LOG: ◯ ◯ ◯ ◯ 1 Gallon or four 32-ounce tumblers

FOOD LOG

DATE:_____

	FOOD	TIME	CALORIES	NOTES
Breakfast *(300 calories)*				
Snack *(50 calories)*				
Lunch *(300 calories)*				
Snack *(150 calories)*				
Dinner *(300 calories)*				
Snack *(100 calories)*				

WATER LOG: ⬤ ⬤ ⬤ ⬤   1 Gallon or four 32-ounce tumblers

MEASUREMENTS

DATE:_____

Body Weight:_____

Body Fat Percentage:_____

MEASUREMENTS

Waist:_____
(2" above navel)

Left Thigh:_____
(just below the buttocks crease)

Waist:_____
(at navel)

Right Thigh:_____
(just below the buttocks crease)

Waist:_____
(2" below navel)

Left Upper Arm:_____
(hanging in middle)

Hips:_____
(largest protrusion)

Right Upper Arm:_____
(hanging in middle)

ADDITIONAL NOTES: _____

_____

_____

_____

_____

_____

_____

_____

_____

_____

_____

_____

_____

YOUR WEEK AT A GLANCE

DAY	WORKOUT	MINUTES
1	Strength Training Workout 1 + After-Dinner Walk	20 + 30
2	After-Dinner Walk	30
3	After-Dinner Walk	30
4	Strength Training Workout 2 + After-Dinner Walk	20 + 30
5	After-Dinner Walk	30
6	After-Dinner Walk	30
7	After-Dinner Walk	30

What You'll Do This Week

EXERCISE

Day 1: Perform the 15-15-15 style, followed by 8 regular reps of each exercise.

Day 4: Perform one 15-15-15 rep, followed by 8 regular reps of each exercise.

NUTRITION

Your calories should be 1,200 per day. Remember to keep individual meals in the 300-calorie range and snacks between 50 and 100 calories.

Belly Toning Tip

TEAM UP, SLIM DOWN You ran around with pals when you were a kid, and there's good reason to keep that up: In one study, women who trained with a skilled partner increased their workout time by as much as 200 percent. Exercising with a partner makes you more accountable (you know she'll be mad if you bail) and less likely to quit early (chatting about celebrity gossip is always a helpful distraction). Plus, training with someone else increases the range of options for exercises you have to choose from, which can help keep your workouts interesting.

EXCUSE-PROOF YOUR WEEK

Congrats, you're halfway through your first 6 weeks of the Flat Belly Break-through program! By now you've probably made some tough calls when it came to sticking to the diet (ditching happy hour, nixing dessert, etc.). But hey, hard work pays off! Need help? Here's a little more motivation.

Lose Weight, Not Money

When you're on a diet, you expect your stomach to be on the empty side—not your wallet. But researchers at the University of Washington found that the cost of healthy, nutrient-dense foods such as whole grains and lean meats has increased nearly 30 percent in the past 4 years, while candy and soft drinks have gone up only 15 percent.

One money-saving tactic: Eat less meat. "Meat is one of the priciest items on a grocery bill, and most Americans eat more of it than they should," says Dawn Jackson Blatner, RD, a spokesperson for the American Dietetic Association and the author of *The Flexitarian Diet*. Plus, meat is a source of excess calories and saturated fat.

Most women can slash around 15 percent of their daily calories by sticking to one or two servings of meat a day, estimates Blatner. Fill the void with fiber-rich foods such as beans, oatmeal, and brown rice, plus hearty veggies such as portobello mushrooms and eggplant. All of these will fill you up for a fraction of the calories and cash.

EXERCISE LOG

Strength Training Workouts

Do $1^1/_2$ slow reps of each move below in 15-second, 15-second, 15-second negative-accentuated style, followed immediately by 8 to 12 regular-speed reps. When you can do 12 reps in good form, move to a harder hand position, starting on pages 94 and 95 of *Flat Belly Breakthrough*. Record your style and number of good-form reps between 8 and 12. The Body Weight Squat can be made more difficult by holding a dumbbell in your hands goblet-style.

MOVE	WORKOUT 1	WORKOUT 2
	DAY/DATE:	DAY/DATE:
Forward Crunch	Reps: 8 to 12	Reps: 8 to 12
Oblique Crunch (right and left)	R: Reps: 8 to 12 L: Reps: 8 to 12	R: Reps: 8 to 12 L: Reps: 8 to 12
V-Crunch	Reps: 8 to 12	Reps: 8 to 12
Pushup	Reps: 8 to 12	Reps: 8 to 12
Body Weight Squat	Reps: 8 to 12	Reps: 8 to 12
Dumbbell Curl	Reps: 8 to 12	Reps: 8 to 12

After-Dinner Walking Log

M:_____ TU:_____ W:_____ TH:_____ F:_____ SA: _____ SU:_____

SLEEP LOG

DATE:_____

DAY	BEDTIME	WAKING TIME	SLEEP QUALITY	NOTES
Monday				
Tuesday				
Wednesday				
Thursday				
Friday				
Saturday				
Sunday				

Sleep Less, Gain More

If you're one of the more than 21 million Americans with a nontraditional work schedule, you may have a tougher time keeping pounds at bay. Less-than-stellar sleep can lower levels of calming, appetite-suppressing hormones and raise stress and hunger-inducing ones. W. Christopher Winter, MD, medical director of the Martha Jefferson Hospital Sleep Medicine Center in Charlottesville, Virginia, offers this advice:

Lay off caffeine: While a morning cup of coffee is fine, avoiding caffeine for at least four hours before you head to bed can help you snooze more soundly.

Be shady: If you drive home in daylight, wear sunglasses. "Walk out of work into tons of light and your brain says, 'You should be awake.' This makes it harder to fall asleep," he says.

Supplement sparingly: Popping sleep-inducing melatonin can help you acclimate to a new schedule, but don't use it every night, and be sure to talk to a sleep-medicine specialist before taking it.

FOOD LOG

DATE:_____

	FOOD	TIME	CALORIES	NOTES
Breakfast (300 calories)				
Snack (50 calories)				
Lunch (300 calories)				
Snack (150 calories)				
Dinner (300 calories)				
Snack (100 calories)				

WATER LOG: ◯ ◯ ◯ ◯   1 Gallon or four 32-ounce tumblers

FOOD LOG

DATE:_____

	FOOD	TIME	CALORIES	NOTES
Breakfast (300 calories)				
Snack (50 calories)				
Lunch (300 calories)				
Snack (150 calories)				
Dinner (300 calories)				
Snack (100 calories)				

WATER LOG: ○ ○ ○ ○   1 Gallon or four 32-ounce tumblers

FOOD LOG

DATE:_____

	FOOD	TIME	CALORIES	NOTES
Breakfast *(300 calories)*				
Snack *(50 calories)*				
Lunch *(300 calories)*				
Snack *(150 calories)*				
Dinner *(300 calories)*				
Snack *(100 calories)*				

WATER LOG: ◯   ◯   ◯   ◯   1 Gallon or four 32-ounce tumblers

FOOD LOG

DATE:_____

	FOOD	TIME	CALORIES	NOTES
Breakfast *(300 calories)*				
Snack *(50 calories)*				
Lunch *(300 calories)*				
Snack *(150 calories)*				
Dinner *(300 calories)*				
Snack *(100 calories)*				

WATER LOG: ◯ ◯ ◯ ◯   1 Gallon or four 32-ounce tumblers

FOOD LOG

DATE:_____

	FOOD	TIME	CALORIES	NOTES
Breakfast *(300 calories)*				
Snack *(50 calories)*				
Lunch *(300 calories)*				
Snack *(150 calories)*				
Dinner *(300 calories)*				
Snack *(100 calories)*				

WATER LOG: ◯ ◯ ◯ ◯   1 Gallon or four 32-ounce tumblers

FOOD LOG

DATE:_____

	FOOD	TIME	CALORIES	NOTES
Breakfast *(300 calories)*				
Snack *(50 calories)*				
Lunch *(300 calories)*				
Snack *(150 calories)*				
Dinner *(300 calories)*				
Snack *(100 calories)*				

WATER LOG: ◯ ◯ ◯ ◯   1 Gallon or four 32-ounce tumblers

FOOD LOG

DATE:_____

	FOOD	TIME	CALORIES	NOTES
Breakfast (300 calories)				
Snack (50 calories)				
Lunch (300 calories)				
Snack (150 calories)				
Dinner (300 calories)				
Snack (100 calories)				

WATER LOG: ◯ ◯ ◯ ◯   1 Gallon or four 32-ounce tumblers

MEASUREMENTS

Body Weight:_____   Body Fat Percentage:_____

MEASUREMENTS

Waist:_____   Left Thigh:_____
(2" above navel)   *(just below the buttocks crease)*

Waist:_____   Right Thigh:_____
(at navel)   *(just below the buttocks crease)*

Waist:_____   Left Upper Arm:_____
(2" below navel)   *(hanging in middle)*

Hips:_____   Right Upper Arm:_____
(largest protrusion)   *(hanging in middle)*

ADDITIONAL NOTES: _____

_____

_____

_____

_____

_____

_____

_____

_____

_____

_____

_____

_____

YOUR WEEK AT A GLANCE

DAY	WORKOUT	MINUTES
1	Strength Training Workout 1 + After-Dinner Walk	20 + 30
2	After-Dinner Walk	30
3	After-Dinner Walk	30
4	Strength Training Workout 2 + After-Dinner Walk	20 + 30
5	After-Dinner Walk	30
6	After-Dinner Walk	30
7	After-Dinner Walk	30

What You'll Do This Week

EXERCISE

Day 1: This week you'll add a new move, the dumbbell overhead press, to your workouts. Perform the 15-15-15 style, followed by 8 to 12 regular reps for each exercise.

Day 4: Perform the 15-15-15 style, followed by 8 to 12 regular reps for each exercise.

NUTRITION

It's crunch time! Finish these last 2 weeks strong, strictly following your 1,100 calorie per day plan. Each meal should be balanced with 50 percent carbs, 25 percent fat, and 25 percent protein.

Belly Toning Tip

UPGRADE YOUR POST-WORKOUT SNACK: Sports scientists have long advocated having a bite after exercising to help promote muscle repair. An even more compelling reason: less belly fat. Exercise activates cortisol, a stress hormone that gives you that extra surge to push until the end of spin class, says Stacy Sims, PhD, an exercise physiologist and nutrition scientist at the Stanford School of Medicine's Prevention Research Center in Palo Alto, California. But lingering in that state for too long can backfire. Cortisol not only inhibits the muscle-repair process but also alters your metabolism so that your body stores more calories

EXCUSE-PROOF YOUR WEEK

In the home stretch, temptation lurks around every corner. Finish strong this week and next—you may be surprised how many healthy habits now come as second nature.

Lose Weight, Not Your Lifestyle

Watching your waistline doesn't mean you have to become a recluse who spends every spare moment on the elliptical machine. In fact, an all-or-nothing approach is counterproductive. "Many women make changes they'll never be able to stick with—like eating nothing but raw food or vowing to go for a run at 5 a.m. every day—and set themselves up for failure," says Donald Hensrud, MD. "Total deprivation doesn't work."

He advocates skipping extreme regimens in favor of small changes. When he asked a group of overweight study subjects to make several small lifestyle shifts—such as eating breakfast, having as many veggies as they'd like with each meal, and watching TV for only as long as they'd exercised that day—they dropped an average of 8 pounds in 2 weeks. "When you combine a bunch of little strategies, the cumulative effect can be huge, and you won't feel as if you've given up your entire life to be slim."

as fat (typically in the abdominal region) instead of burning them off. Luckily, chowing down on some protein within 30 minutes after your workout will prevent these deleterious effects, says Sims, who suggests eating a hard-boiled egg or substituting low-fat milk for the fruit juice in your smoothie. Even Starbucks fans are in luck: With a nonfat mocha latte, you'll get the cortisol antidote (protein) from the milk, plus a secret weapon—caffeine. One study found that, when ingested with carbs (the chocolate, in this case), caffeine increased muscles' energy production 66 percent more than carbs alone.

Strength Training Workouts

Do $1^1/_2$ slow reps of each move below in 15-second, 15-second, 15-second negative-accentuated style, followed immediately by 8 to 12 regular-speed reps. When you can do 12 reps in good form, move to a harder hand position, as shown on pages 94 and 95 of *Flat Belly Breakthrough*. Record your style and number of good-form reps between 8 and 12. The Body Weight Squat can be made more difficult by holding a dumbbell in your hands goblet-style.

MOVE	WORKOUT 1	WORKOUT 2
	DAY/DATE:	DAY/DATE:
Forward Crunch	Reps: 8 to 12	Reps: 8 to 12
Oblique Crunch (right and left)	R: Reps: 8 to 12 L: Reps: 8 to 12	R: Reps: 8 to 12 L: Reps: 8 to 12
V-Crunch	Reps: 8 to 12	Reps: 8 to 12
Pushup	Reps: 8 to 12	Reps: 8 to 12
Body Weight Squat	Reps: 8 to 12	Reps: 8 to 12
Dumbbell Curl	Reps: 8 to 12	Reps: 8 to 12
Dumbbell Overhead Press	Reps: 8 to 12	Reps: 8 to 12

After-Dinner Walking Log

M:_____   TU:_____   W:_____   TH:_____   F:_____   SA: _____   SU:_____

SLEEP LOG

DATE:_____

DAY	BEDTIME	WAKING TIME	SLEEP QUALITY	NOTES
Monday				
Tuesday				
Wednesday				
Thursday				
Friday				
Saturday				
Sunday				

Rise and Actually Shine

Whether you've skimped on sleep or scored a solid 8 hours, mornings can be, in a word, brutal. Blame your brain: Everyone is hardwired to be either a night owl or an early bird—and only 15 percent of people are natural-born larks. Not part of that lucky minority? You can still beat biology.

Sip water before coffee: After a long stretch in the sack without fluids, your body is thirsty, which can lead to brain fog, per a University of Connecticut study. Right after your dreaded alarm goes off, gulp down a tall glass of H_2O; it may help clear the cobwebs from your mind and improve your mood.

Next, give yourself a squeeze, literally: Research shows that self-administered acupressure pumps up mental alertness in the morning. Using a clockwise motion, massage the pressure point between your thumb and your forefinger on each hand for 2 minutes; then switch to a counterclockwise motion for 2 minutes.

Once you're out of bed, reach for some rosemary: A study in the *International Journal of Neuroscience* found that sniffing the herb promotes alertness.

FOOD LOG

DATE:_____

	FOOD	TIME	CALORIES	NOTES
Breakfast *(300 calories)*				
Snack *(50 calories)*				
Lunch *(300 calories)*				
Snack *(50 calories)*				
Dinner *(300 calories)*				
Snack *(100 calories)*				

WATER LOG: ◯ ◯ ◯ ◯   1 Gallon or four 32-ounce tumblers

FOOD LOG

DATE:_____

	FOOD	TIME	CALORIES	NOTES
Breakfast *(300 calories)*				
Snack *(50 calories)*				
Lunch *(300 calories)*				
Snack *(50 calories)*				
Dinner *(300 calories)*				
Snack *(100 calories)*				

WATER LOG: ◯ ◯ ◯ ◯   1 Gallon or four 32-ounce tumblers

FOOD LOG

DATE:_____

	FOOD	TIME	CALORIES	NOTES
Breakfast *(300 calories)*				
Snack *(50 calories)*				
Lunch *(300 calories)*				
Snack *(50 calories)*				
Dinner *(300 calories)*				
Snack *(100 calories)*				

WATER LOG: ◯ ◯ ◯ ◯   1 Gallon or four 32-ounce tumblers

FOOD LOG

DATE:_____

	FOOD	TIME	CALORIES	NOTES
Breakfast (300 calories)				
Snack (50 calories)				
Lunch (300 calories)				
Snack (50 calories)				
Dinner (300 calories)				
Snack (100 calories)				

WATER LOG: ○ ○ ○ ○   1 Gallon or four 32-ounce tumblers

FOOD LOG

DATE:_____

	FOOD	TIME	CALORIES	NOTES
Breakfast *(300 calories)*				
Snack *(50 calories)*				
Lunch *(300 calories)*				
Snack *(50 calories)*				
Dinner *(300 calories)*				
Snack *(100 calories)*				

WATER LOG: ◯ ◯ ◯ ◯   1 Gallon or four 32-ounce tumblers

FOOD LOG

DATE:_____

	FOOD	TIME	CALORIES	NOTES
Breakfast *(300 calories)*				
Snack *(50 calories)*				
Lunch *(300 calories)*				
Snack *(50 calories)*				
Dinner *(300 calories)*				
Snack *(100 calories)*				

WATER LOG: ◯ ◯ ◯ ◯   1 Gallon or four 32-ounce tumblers

FOOD LOG

DATE:_____

	FOOD	TIME	CALORIES	NOTES
Breakfast *(300 calories)*				
Snack *(50 calories)*				
Lunch *(300 calories)*				
Snack *(50 calories)*				
Dinner *(300 calories)*				
Snack *(100 calories)*				

WATER LOG: ◯ ◯ ◯ ◯   1 Gallon or four 32-ounce tumblers

MEASUREMENTS

DATE:_____

Body Weight:_____   Body Fat Percentage:_____

MEASUREMENTS

Waist:_____
(2" above navel)

Waist:_____
(at navel)

Waist:_____
(2" below navel)

Hips:_____
(largest protrusion)

Left Thigh:_____
(just below the buttocks crease)

Right Thigh:_____
(just below the buttocks crease)

Left Upper Arm:_____
(hanging in middle)

Right Upper Arm:_____
(hanging in middle)

ADDITIONAL NOTES: _____

_____

_____

_____

_____

_____

_____

_____

_____

_____

_____

_____

_____

Week 6

YOUR WEEK AT A GLANCE

DAY	WORKOUT	MINUTES
1	Strength Training Workout 1 + After-Dinner Walk	20 + 30
2	After-Dinner Walk	30
3	After-Dinner Walk	30
4	Strength Training Workout 2 + After-Dinner Walk	20 + 30
5	After-Dinner Walk	30
6	After-Dinner Walk	30
7	After-Dinner Walk	30

What You'll Do This Week

EXERCISE

Day 1: Perform the 15-15-15 style, followed by 8 to 12 regular reps for each exercise.

Day 4: Perform the 15-15-15 style, followed by 8 to 12 regular reps for each exercise.

NUTRITION

It's your last week of cycle one! If you find your weight loss stalled, try varying your meal times to stoke your fat burn.

Belly Toning Tip

THOUGHT CONTROL: The best way to quell a craving, research shows, is to focus on the positive payoffs of avoiding the food (like debuting a new bikini) rather than dwelling on the downsides of pigging out. According to study author Sonja Yokum, PhD, practicing the pattern helps make it habit.

EXCUSE-PROOF YOUR WEEK

You made it to Week 6! That means you've powered through cravings, made after-dinner walking a daily habit, torched calories with negative-accentuated training, and logged your success along the way. In the final week, sticking to the plan for 7 more days will help you polish off your new, improved self! Be proud of how far you've come and stay positive to finish the program strong.

Lose Weight, Love Your Belly

Fact of life: As we age, our bodies change, especially our bellies. Sure, it's hard to love those love handles, but if you appreciate your midsection, lumps and all, you're more likely to adopt the healthy habits that can keep it tightened and toned, says Ann Kearney-Cooke, PhD, women's health and wellness expert. Here's a few ways to embrace your weight loss, and how to wear your new weight proud.

Stop comparing yourself to a fantasy: Those bare-abbed goddesses in the glossies are often the result of the fanciest digital fixes. "We've become conditioned to want things that aren't natural," says Sarah Maria, a body image expert and the author of *Love Your Body, Love Your Life*. "Teach yourself to value a natural body. Discover the beauty that comes from being alive."

Stop belly bashing: "If you think, Ugh, my belly is gross, ask yourself: Would I ever say that to a good friend?" says Vivian Diller, PhD, the author of *Face It: What Women Really Feel As Their Looks Change*. Instead, think of the ways your abdomen works for you, from keeping your immune system functioning well to gestating babies. "Gratitude is a great antidote to unhappiness," says Dr. Diller.

Project forward: "Ten years from now you may really appreciate the belly you have today," says Dr. Diller. "Why not just appreciate it now?"

Week 6

EXERCISE LOG

DATE:_____

Strength Training Workouts

Do $1^1/_2$ slow reps of each move below in 15-second, 15-second, 15-second negative-accentuated style, followed immediately by 8 to 12 regular-speed reps. When you can do 12 reps in good form, move to a harder hand position, as shown on pages 94 and 95 of *Flat Belly Breakthrough*. Record your style and number of good-form reps between 8 and 12. The Body Weight Squat can be made more difficult by holding a dumbbell in your hands goblet-style.

MOVE	WORKOUT 1	WORKOUT 2
	DAY/DATE:	DAY/DATE:
Forward Crunch	Reps: 8 to 12	Reps: 8 to 12
Oblique Crunch (right and left)	R: Reps: 8 to 12 L: Reps: 8 to 12	R: Reps: 8 to 12 L: Reps: 8 to 12
V-Crunch	Reps: 8 to 12	Reps: 8 to 12
Pushup	Reps: 8 to 12	Reps: 8 to 12
Body Weight Squat	Reps: 8 to 12	Reps: 8 to 12
Dumbbell Curl	Reps: 8 to 12	Reps: 8 to 12
Dumbbell Overhead Press	Reps: 8 to 12	Reps: 8 to 12

After-Dinner Walking Log

M:_____ TU:_____ W:_____ TH:_____ F:_____ SA: _____ SU:_____

SLEEP LOG

DATE:_____

DAY	BEDTIME	WAKING TIME	SLEEP QUALITY	NOTES
Monday				
Tuesday				
Wednesday				
Thursday				
Friday				
Saturday				
Sunday				

Try a New Bedtime Snack

In a small study, participants who had two kiwifruit each night before bed went to sleep faster and slept longer. Raw kiwi contains high levels of serotonin and folate, both of which could contribute to the improved z's.

FOOD LOG

DATE:_____

	FOOD	TIME	CALORIES	NOTES
Breakfast (300 calories)				
Snack (50 calories)				
Lunch (300 calories)				
Snack (50 calories)				
Dinner (300 calories)				
Snack (100 calories)				

WATER LOG: ◯ ◯ ◯ ◯   1 Gallon or four 32-ounce tumblers

FOOD LOG

DATE:_____

	FOOD	TIME	CALORIES	NOTES
Breakfast *(300 calories)*				
Snack *(50 calories)*				
Lunch *(300 calories)*				
Snack *(50 calories)*				
Dinner *(300 calories)*				
Snack *(100 calories)*				

WATER LOG: ◯ ◯ ◯ ◯   1 Gallon or four 32-ounce tumblers

FOOD LOG

DATE:_____

	FOOD	TIME	CALORIES	NOTES
Breakfast (300 calories)				
Snack (50 calories)				
Lunch (300 calories)				
Snack (50 calories)				
Dinner (300 calories)				
Snack (100 calories)				

WATER LOG: ○ ○ ○ ○   1 Gallon or four 32-ounce tumblers

FOOD LOG

DATE:_____

	FOOD	TIME	CALORIES	NOTES
Breakfast *(300 calories)*				
Snack *(50 calories)*				
Lunch *(300 calories)*				
Snack *(50 calories)*				
Dinner *(300 calories)*				
Snack *(100 calories)*				

WATER LOG: ◯ ◯ ◯ ◯   1 Gallon or four 32-ounce tumblers

FOOD LOG

DATE:_____

	FOOD	TIME	CALORIES	NOTES
Breakfast *(300 calories)*				
Snack *(50 calories)*				
Lunch *(300 calories)*				
Snack *(50 calories)*				
Dinner *(300 calories)*				
Snack *(100 calories)*				

WATER LOG: ◯ ◯ ◯ ◯   1 Gallon or four 32-ounce tumblers

FOOD LOG

DATE:_____

	FOOD	TIME	CALORIES	NOTES
Breakfast *(300 calories)*				
Snack *(50 calories)*				
Lunch *(300 calories)*				
Snack *(50 calories)*				
Dinner *(300 calories)*				
Snack *(100 calories)*				

WATER LOG: ◯ ◯ ◯ ◯   1 Gallon or four 32-ounce tumblers

FOOD LOG

DATE:_____

	FOOD	TIME	CALORIES	NOTES
Breakfast *(300 calories)*				
Snack *(50 calories)*				
Lunch *(300 calories)*				
Snack *(50 calories)*				
Dinner *(300 calories)*				
Snack *(100 calories)*				

WATER LOG: ◯ ◯ ◯ ◯ 1 Gallon or four 32-ounce tumblers

MEASUREMENTS

Body Weight:_____   Body Fat Percentage:_____

MEASUREMENTS

Waist:_____   Left Thigh:_____
(2" above navel)   *(just below the buttocks crease)*

Waist:_____   Right Thigh:_____
(at navel)   *(just below the buttocks crease)*

Waist:_____   Left Upper Arm:_____
(2" below navel)   *(hanging in middle)*

Hips:_____   Right Upper Arm:_____
(largest protrusion)   *(hanging in middle)*

ADDITIONAL NOTES: _____

_____

_____

_____

_____

_____

_____

_____

_____

_____

_____

_____

_____

Lose Weight, Feel Great GROCERY GUIDE

When you first step inside the grocery store, you have every intention of filling it up with the ingredients you need to make nutritious meals and snacks for the entire week. But somehow, what ends up in your cart is usually a mixed bag, health-wise.

Luckily you're one step ahead of the game with this journal in your possession. This special section is stocked with all the info you need to pick up the most wholesome foods possible each week. Tips and tricks from the Flat Belly Breakthrough test panelists, and expert nutritionists will help you bypass the cookie aisle and foolproof your weight loss for good!

GRAB A BASKET

A study in the *Journal of Marketing Research* shows that shopping with a basket instead of a cart makes you nearly seven times more likely to purchase vice foods such as candy and chocolate. The researchers say that curling your arm inward to carry a basket increases your desire to embrace instant rewards, such as sweet foods. With a cart, you tend to extend your arm—a motion associated with avoiding negative outcomes. That makes you more likely to shop smart.

Lesson one: Nix your trips down the snack aisle and cruise the outside perimeter. That's where most grocery stores house healthy, fresh options. See how easy that was? Now, let's get started!

Anatomy of a Healthy Kitchen

Sure, you know how to eat healthfully. So why do you have moments of double-fudge-brownie-induced weakness? New research in the realm of behavioral economics, the study of how and why we make decisions, shows how much our surroundings matter. Brian Wansink, PhD, director of the Cornell University Food and Brand Lab, helped us design a kitchen that maximizes your potential for proper eating.

Put healthy food at eye level in clear containers. You're about three times more likely to eat the first item you see than something you have to dig out.

Pick the right plates. People serve 18 percent more on dishes that match the food's color and 22 percent more on large plates, regardless of hunger, so opt for small (10-inch) plates that contrast with the color of your food.

Keep that fruit bowl stocked. The smell of citrus helps suppress appetite, so having lemons, oranges, or grapefruit within smelling distance may keep you from overdoing it.

Use a smaller serving fork. To avoid dishing out oversize portions, serve with regular tableware rather than jumbo utensils.

COOK MORE, WEIGH LESS

Your skillet makes a remarkable slim-down weapon. A recent study found that people who made dinner 6 or 7 nights a week ate an average of 137 fewer calories, 3 grams less fat, and 16 grams less sugar daily than those who cooked once weekly or not at all—no surprise, given that most restaurant fare is supersized and carb-packed. More unexpectedly, home cooks also ate fewer calories when they did dine out, which suggests that healthy tastes culled at the stove can carry over no matter where you eat.

Source: *Public Health Nutrition*

Curb your clutter. Keeping the table clear means you'll actually sit down to it. Both adults and kids tend to have lower BMIs if they eat meals together around the table. The positive effect of socializing during dinner seems to override the desire to overeat.

You Are Where You Eat

Where you eat a meal plays a surprising role in whether you'll overeat. In a recent Cornell University study, half of the diners at a Hardee's restaurant were randomly selected to eat in a temporary fine-dining area, while the rest ate in the regular fast-food setting. The results: Diners in the nicer room ate roughly 133 fewer calories, spent nearly 5 percent more time eating, and rated the food quality 1.5 points higher on a 10-point scale, despite the fact that both groups had the same menu choices. You can mimic these healthy effects by creating a sacred place for eating, says Junelle Lupiani, RD, a weight management specialist at Miraval Resort and Spa in Tucson. Here's how.

Dim the Lights

The researchers dimmed their pop-up dining room using curtains and provided lighting with candles and soft lights. "When there is low lighting, people tend to linger over their food longer," says Kelly Grant, RD, a nutritionist at Canyon Ranch health resort in Tucson.

Add Some Green

At spas, dining areas often overlook gardens. At home, set an indoor mini-herb or microgreens garden in view of the table to encourage thoughtful eating. As you dig into your salad, visualize the process of food growing, maturing, and finally arriving at your table, Grant suggests.

Play It Slow

Make Michael Bublé your dinner date. "We played soft jazz in the background," says study coauthor Koert van Ittersum. "This may have helped people relax and slow down their pace." Play something soothing at a low volume. At the end of every song, to prevent overindulging, evaluate how full you feel.

Your Grocery Guide: Shop for Success Each Week

Grocery shopping is less of a drag if you can avoid screaming kids and impulse buys. We'll help with one of those things.

On Your Way There

Eat a Fuji. Shoppers who gobbled an apple before a grocery run bought 28 percent more fruits and veggies than those who had a cookie, per the Cornell Food and Brand Lab.

Down the Aisles

Stick to your must-buy list as you fill up your eco-friendly tote. A Harvard Business School study found that people may reward themselves for being green by buying more junk food.

At the Checkout

Resist the candy urge. According to a recent study, guilty splurges happen at the end of a trip. Make the produce section your last stop before checking out and you'll be less likely to cave at the register.

BONUS: Avoid Lines

The longer you're exposed to tempting snacks at the checkout, the more likely you are to succumb to them, say University of Arizona researchers. Avoid the wait by shopping during off-peak hours, such as the middle of the week or late at night.

INSTANT TUMMY TONER: CHERRIES

Studies show that anthocyanins squelch muscle inflammation and the pain that can come with having an overzealous trainer. Cherries are full of 'em. Stash a couple dozen (fresh or dried) in your bag to have after your last set.

Your Lose Weight, Feel Great Basic Shopping List

Because you have your journal on hand at all times for easy, on-the-go logging, we decided to make sure you also have a fail-safe grocery list with you as well. Next time you get to the store only to discover you left your list at home, just flip to this page and review the basics. Keep your cupboards stocked with healthy choices and you'll be less likely to fall off track!

Condiments

Mustard (spicy or classic)

Whole, organic, unsalted almonds

Whole, organic, unsalted cashews

Black tea

Coffee

Grains

Whole-wheat bagels

Whole-wheat bread

Produce

Red apples (3-inch diameters)

Dried plums

Organic Romaine lettuce (locally grown if possible)

Beefsteak tomatoes

Dairy

Whipped cream cheese

Reduced-fat Colby-Jack cheese, sliced

Light yogurt, flavored

Meat and Vegetables

White turkey meat, thinly sliced

Ham, thinly sliced

Frozen Foods

Lean Cuisine Orange Chicken

Lean Cuisine Lemon Pepper Fish

Michelina's Lean Gourmet Three Cheese Ziti Marinara

Dressed for Success

Whip up your own salad dressing using roughly three parts oil to one part vinegar, or half oil and half lime or lemon juice.

Flavor Saviors: Seasonings for Success

Rescue your taste buds from bland dishes. These spices and sauces are easy, low-calorie ways to amp up your meals and add variety to your daily dishes.

Smoked Paprika

Ground from smoke-dried Spanish peppers, this potent powder delivers a serious dose of earthiness.

TIP: Add it to chicken or nuts before roasting; sprinkle on broiled fish, sautéed potatoes, and popcorn; use it to add depth to chili.

Chile-Garlic Sauce

Sriracha steals all the attention, but this well-balanced sauce blends the bite of garlic with the kick of ground red jalapeños.

TIP: Its balanced heat is awesome atop eggs or in a marinade for pork or chicken wings.

Dijon Mustard

Dijon packs acidity to cut through rich, dense dishes.

TIP: Add a spoonful to homemade mac and cheese; toss with carrots and a bit of honey prior to roasting; or spread on toasted bread as part of a killer ham or turkey sandwich.

Salsa

Loaded with heat and fresh flavor, salsa is a ready-to-go sauce.

TIP: Cook eggs in a simmering pan of salsa; stir a couple of tablespoon into chicken soup mix and top with tortilla chips for a simple Mexican soup; stir-fry shrimp with salsa and serve over rice and beans.

BBQ Sauce

Spicy, sweet, tangy, smoky—barbecue sauce boasts a range of flavors few condiments can beat.

TIP: Spike vinaigrette with it and dress a salad of romaine, Cotija cheese, pico de gallo, beans, and grilled chicken.

Equalize Your Energy:
A Perfect Day of Eating

The Flat Belly Breakthrough program emphasizes the importance of balanced nutrition and energy from carb-rich meals. But recent trends in food sciences often place emphasis on protein-heavy diets. Here's the deal with the lean protein love affair: Americans love gorging on protein come dinnertime, but parceling it out over the day is a better bet, finds a recent study in the *Journal of Nutrition.*

People who ate about 30 grams of protein at each meal—breakfast, lunch, and dinner—had a 25 percent boost in building lean muscle, compared with those who ate the same total amount but skimped in the morning and loaded up at night.

"Balancing out your protein intake optimizes muscle protein synthesis at more points throughout the day, not just at night," says lead study author Doug Paddon-Jones, a professor at the University of Texas Medical Branch at Galveston. That can help you retain muscle you might otherwise forfeit to age, so spread the protein love around.

Breakfast

2 scrambled eggs, $\frac{1}{2}$ cup low-fat cottage cheese, and 1 cup cubed melon

Protein: 28 grams

Lunch

2 cups spinach topped with 3 ounces grilled chicken and $\frac{1}{2}$ avocado

Protein: 30 grams

Dinner

4 ounces salmon fillet, 10 asparagus spears, and 1 medium baked
sweet potato

Protein: 28 grams

Anatomy of a Healthy Breakfast

The perfect breakfast relies on a simple formula you've heard before: Every meal should be a happy combo of high-fiber carbs, lean protein, and healthy fats. Here's exactly how that breaks down in the morning:

1. Make half your breakfast high-fiber carbs such as two slices of sprouted-grain toast and a medium orange, $\frac{1}{2}$ cup of oatmeal with a sliced banana, one small sweet potato with $\frac{1}{2}$ cup of beans, or a smoothie made with a banana and 1 cup each of chopped kale and chopped strawberries. Fiber is superfilling and provides long-lasting energy. Aim for about 50 grams of fiber-rich carbs.

2. Add a shot of protein such as 1 cup of fat-free Greek yogurt, two eggs, three ounces of smoked salmon, $\frac{1}{2}$ cup of tofu, four slices of tempeh bacon, or a scoop of protein powder. Protein should make up about a quarter of your meal, or 25 grams, to help keep you fuller longer, stabilize blood sugar, and blunt cravings.

3. Finish with a fat such as 1 tablespoon of almond butter, 2 teaspoons of olive or flaxseed oil, or a quarter of an avocado. These healthy fats don't just make breakfast taste better but also give the meal some staying power in your stomach. Aim to make fat 20 to 25 percent of your calories, or about 10 grams. Most of that should be mono- or polyunsaturated fats, but 2 or 3 grams of saturated fat, like that found in two eggs, is fine, too.

Breakfast Means Morning, Not Afternoon

You don't have to eat the minute you wake up, but try to get something in your stomach within an hour or two of rising. When you wait too long, your metabolism starts to slow down in an effort to conserve fuel. You're also more likely to feel ravenous by midmorning.

And that's really the point: Fill up on a wholesome breakfast that follows our formula and you won't have room for the type of fare that used to sabotage your morning—processed cereals, bacon and sausage (often high in saturated fat and heart-unhealthy nitrites), packaged baked goods, and sugary instant oatmeal.

You don't have to rule out the sweet stuff completely. Just make it less than 5 grams, a light pour. After all, there's nothing more satisfying than a teaspoon of honey on top of your toast or a drizzle of maple syrup on your oatmeal—especially when you know breakfast is setting you up to eat less later on.

Anatomy of a Healthy Lunch

Make it green. Midday meals can be so snooze-worthy. And salads? Yawn. Try these exciting options that revamp how you eat your greens—they taste delicious and are a snap to pack when you're on the go.

Collard Green Wraps

Think of collards as carb-free tortillas. Remove their stiff backbones and they become pliable, while still holding up to travel (no tearing or sogginess) better than flimsier greens. Add flavor by filling them with crumbly cheeses mixed with crisp vegetables and bright herbs.

12:38 p.m. The optimal time to eat lunch to maximize weight loss, according to a recent survey by diet company Forza Supplements.

With a paring knife, shave the thick spine from two collard leaves, being careful not to cut into the leaves. Flip them over and spread 2 tablespoons hummus on each wrap. Top each with one sliced hard-boiled egg, 1 tablespoon grated carrots, one sliced radish, and 1½ tablespoons chopped roasted red peppers. Sprinkle each with ½ tablespoon chopped parsley and ½ tablespoon crumbled feta, then fold them like burritos.

Makes 1 serving: 320 calories, 21 g protein, 19 g carbs, 19 g fat, 6 g saturated fat, 8 g fiber, 520 mg sodium

Salad in a Jar

Why bother with a plate when you can make, carry, and eat your lunch from a single vessel? The dressing-on-the-bottom approach keeps your veggies crunchy and lettuce crisp until the moment you're ready to enjoy. Then a few flips of the jar will coat everything nicely—genius.

In the bottom of a large jar, combine 1 tablespoon olive oil, 1 teaspoon each of red wine vinegar and Dijon mustard, and ½ teaspoon honey. Seal the jar and shake vigorously until the oil and vinegar combine. Layer in ⅓ cup cooked cranberry beans, ⅓ cup sliced radishes, ½ cup cooked freekah (or another chewy whole grain), a pinch of minced tarragon, and 2 tablespoons chopped black olives. Top with 2 tablespoons soft goat cheese. Fill the rest of the jar with ½ cup lightly packed arugula.

Makes 1 serving: 350 calories, 13 g protein, 26 g carbs, 22 g fat, 6 g saturated fat, 8 g fiber, 370 mg sodium

Anatomy of a Healthy Dinner

You've learned the basics of portion control from noshing on Lean Cuisines for dinner, but grown tired of the options? Expand your palate with our top picks for frozen entrées that deliver delicious flavor, while keeping calories in check.

Hilary's Eat Well Adzuki Bean Burger: Hands down, Hilary's is our new favorite meatless patty. She ditches the traditional veggie burger black beans for adzuki, a flavorful Asian variety that's full of folate.

Captain Jack's Seafood Locker Wild Alaskan Sockeye Salmon: You can taste the freshness, and the omega-3s practically pop out of the bright red protein. The only downside? Once you try a taste of Captain Jack's, you'll have a really hard time going back to restaurant salmon.

Amy's Light in Sodium Vegetable Lasagna: Iron and calcium abound in this satisfying frozen meal. It packs 30 percent of your daily vitamin A, too.

Bold Organics Veggie Lovers Pizza: If you're allergic to everything, then this pizza's for you. It's a quick, high-fiber dinner that's big in flavor and free of . . . almost everything else.

Ancient Harvest Quinoa Polenta: Ancient Harvest's prepared version matches the flavor of homemade (but it's so much easier).

Luvo Whole Grain Penne Pasta with Turkey Meatballs: Among the best new products in the freezer aisle, ready-to-eat meals from Luvo taste like a chef prepared them. These turkey meatballs are cleverly bulked up by oatmeal, giving the whole dish 18 grams of protein.

Cappello's Gluten-Free Fettuccine: This unique pasta is free of gluten and grains; instead, it's made from almond flour and cage-free eggs. Rich and Paleo-friendly? We'll twirl our forks to that.

Pacific Organic Creamy Butternut Squash Soup, Light in Sodium: Spice up this subtle soup with a bit of cumin or curry powder and season with a pinch of salt and pepper.

INSTANT TUMMY TONER: LEMON

Squeeze the juice or sprinkle zest over vegetables instead of using extra oil, butter, or salt. You can sauté spinach with just a teaspoon of oil, and then add a little lemon juice for a lot of flavor without a lot of calories.

Applegate The Great Organic Uncured Turkey Hot Dog: With no artificial fillers or preservatives, this flavor-filled organic turkey hot dog blows the competition right off the bun.

DIY Frozen Feasts

Keeping a well-stocked freezer can save you when life gets crazy and making it to the market just isn't going to happen. Frozen veggies are loaded with vitamins, minerals, and fiber—and of course, they don't go bad like fresh produce does (so no guilt if you can't use it all the first couple of days after you buy it).

Besides keeping frozen entrees on hand to keep your portions in check and calories on point, add lean protein and bagged veggies to your freezer as well. That way, you can make easy, nutritious, diet-friendly feasts that you (and your whole family) will be excited to dig in to.

Chicken Stir Fry

Applegate Naturals Grilled Chicken Breast Strips

Birds Eye Pepper Stir Fry

Slice 1 pre-cooked frozen chicken breast, then sauté with 1 teaspoon sesame oil, 1 cup frozen stir-fry veggie mix, and 1 teaspoon soy sauce.

Quinoa Pilaf

Village Harvest Frozen Quinoa

Woodstock Frozen Butternut Squash, diced

Birds Eye Frozen White Pearl Onions

Heat ³/₄ cup frozen butternut squash in microwave for 2 minutes. Meanwhile, sauté ¹/₂ cup frozen quinoa and ¹/₂ cup frozen pearl onions in 1 teaspoon olive oil for 2 minutes, stirring occasionally. Combine all the ingredients in sauté pan, and cook for 1 more minute.

Chicken & Waffles

Applegate Naturals Homestyle Breaded Chicken Breast Tenders

Nature's Path Organic Homestyle Whole-Grain Waffle

Prepare 2 chicken tenders according to package instructions. Meanwhile, toast 1 frozen whole-grain waffle. Top waffle with cooked chicken, and drizzle 1 teaspoon maple syrup over dish.

Snacking Survival Guide

When the day is dragging, your need to nosh on unhealthy foods can go from mild to wild in a matter of minutes. Before one chip turns into an entire bag, see the below tips for ways to manage your cravings by choosing a healthier, more satisfying option or, better yet, derail them completely.

Snacking Pitfalls

Snacking Pitfall #1: You're good all day but pig out at night

You're the Jekyll and Hyde of snacking—restricting calories so much by day that by night you're ravenous. After dinner, you trek back and forth to the fridge. Before you know it, you're cuddled up on the couch with a box of Oreos.

The Fix: Start with a breakfast that's really satisfying—think steel-cut oats, eggs, or Greek-style yogurt. At lunch, combine healthy carbs, protein, and fat. And truly savor your treats. Dean Ornish, MD, the author of *The Spectrum*, does a "chocolate meditation." Take a single piece of the best chocolate you can find and let it dissolve slowly in your mouth, paying attention to the complex flavors. You'll get more pleasure with fewer calories.

Snacking Pitfall #2: You stuff your face before dinner

You're ravenous by the time you get home from work (join the club). You inhale whatever you get your hands on, whether it's healthy or not.

The Fix: "Planning is key," says Patricia Bannan, RD, the author of *Eat Right When Time Is Tight*. Before you get home, eat something light and nourishing to tide you over. If you're starving while you cook, munch on raw veggies such as sugar snap peas. Set yourself up for success by knowing meals you can cook quickly, such as frozen veggies with a rotisserie chicken and microwaveable brown rice.

Snacking Pitfall #3: You can't stop eating in the car

If you feel as though you live in your car, you probably consume a lot of calories there, too. Maybe you wolf down snacks straight out of the bag, with little idea of how much you've inhaled, or you pull into the nearest drive-thru for a shake.

The Fix: Preempt unrestrained noshing by packing portable, calorie-controlled nibbles such as small bags of cashews or an apple. Even half of a PB&J on whole wheat will do the trick. And if those fries are still calling out to you, "drive home via another route so you won't pass your favorite fast-food restaurants," says Janna L. Fikkan, PhD, a health psychologist at Duke Integrative Medicine in Durham, North Carolina. "It doesn't have to be the shortest way home, as long as you avoid the drive-thru."

Snacking Pitfall #4: You work at home

It's just you and the fridge—and nobody watching. Because you have no meetings or structured activities, you can check the mail, toss in a load of laundry, play with the dog—and grab a snack (or two or four).

The Fix: Keep a log of your daily activities, including every time you get up to eat. Chances are, once you see how often you're indulging, you'll be shamed into cutting back. If you still feel the need to snack, eat at the kitchen table—and don't do anything else. Without the distraction of the computer, TV, or newspaper, you'll be much more aware of how often you eat out of habit rather than hunger.

Snacking Pitfall #5: You graze at the office

Between the office candy bowl, the vending machine, and a coworker's home-made brownies, your office probably stocks more snacks than a 7-Eleven. And because you're only nibbling, the calories don't count, right?

The Fix: Launch a counteroffensive by bringing healthy snacks—say, tamari-roasted almonds or dark chocolate—that you actually prefer over the junk. Knowing that these treats are tucked away will give you the strength to resist the disastrous jelly doughnuts. If you know ahead of time that you won't be able to leave your desk at noon, brown-bag it for lunch. With healthy fare within arm's reach, you won't need to raid your colleague's candy jar.

Make a Healthy Swap

The easiest way to get over a breakup is to find a drool-worthy rebound. That tactic might also work for food, according to a study in the *Journal of Consumer Research*. People were able to move on from their go-to treat when they ate a similar-tasting (but healthier) one. Because you're enjoying a comparable flavor, you don't feel deprived, says Rebecca Scritchfield, RD, founder of Capitol Nutrition Group in Washington, DC. Here, she shares some of her favorite stand-ins for common cravings.

When you want sorbet, or fruity ice cream

Reach for frozen grapes, mango, or bananas

When you want pretzels, or potato chips

Reach for veggie chips or roasted chickpeas

When you want chocolate candy bars

Reach for dates stuffed with creamy peanut butter and chocolate chips

When you want french fries

Reach for baked zucchini fries

End Your Mindless Munching

It's not just Paula Deen who'll bulk you up. A new study shows that people eat significantly more when watching any TV show.

Researchers gave 45 subjects a bowl of potato chips for 5 minutes with no TV, and then in front of both Jay Leno's and David Letterman's monologues. Participants ate 41.9 percent more chips during the Leno clip and 44.2 percent more while Letterman was on. "Watching TV while eating causes a distraction, so you're less aware of smells, tastes, and how full you feel," says lead study author Alan Hirsch, MD. "The more engaging the show, the more you'll eat." Chowing tubeside? Serve up the exact portion you plan to eat ahead of time.

Stash a Snack

If you're carrying something that's healthy and portion controlled, you can satisfy the munchies without succumbing to a 500-calorie muffin. Try packing light cheese, raw almonds, a packet of dry cereal, or a piece of fruit in your purse. Need more inspiration? See below.

Seven Snacks with Fewer Than 100 Calories

- 2 (6") corn tortillas + 2 tablespoons salsa
- 1 cup pineapple chunks + 2 tablespoons shredded coconut
- 25 pistachios
- $\frac{1}{2}$ cup Cheerios + $\frac{1}{2}$ cup fat-free milk
- 4 ounces honey Greek-style yogurt
- A handful ($\frac{1}{8}$ cup) of dry-roasted pumpkin seeds
- 5 fresh apricots

10 Time-Saving Healthy Packaged Foods

When there's no time for fresh options, stash these grab-and-go eats for days when you're too busy to slow down. Each packs delicious flavor, without post-meal regret.

Pure Organic Strawberry Apple Fruit & Veggie Strip

Not a bad way to get some of your five-a-day when fresh isn't an option: fruit leathers made from organic, non-GMO fruit and no artificial anything.

Per strip: 50 calories, 0 g protein, 11 g carbs, 0 g fat, 0 g saturated fat, 1 g fiber, 10 mg sodium

Mary's Gone Crackers Super Seed Crackers

Made without gluten or soy, these organic crisps taste a whole lot more substantial than they look, thanks to healthy grains including flaxseeds, brown rice, and quinoa.

Per 13 crackers: 160 calories, 3 g protein, 19 g carbs, 8 g fat, 1 g saturated fat, 3 g fiber, 230 mg sodium

Weight Watchers Light Jalapeño String Cheese

The combo of creamy, reduced-fat mozzarella and fiery jalapeño pleases your palate, while the protein tames your growling tummy.

Per stick: 50 calories, 6 g protein, 1 g carbs, 3 g fat, 0 g fiber, 200 mg sodium

Sunsweet Amaz!n Berry Blend

This resealable bag of dried cranberries, cherries, blueberries, and plums is an antioxidant-packed way to please your sweet tooth anywhere.

Per ¼ cup: 110 calories, 1 g protein, 29 g carbs, 0 g fat, 0 g saturated fat, 2 g fiber, 0 mg sodium

Bumble Bee Prime Fillet Albacore Tuna with Chipotle & Olive Oil

This smoky, spicy-flavored fish is the ideal midday pick-me-up, full of omega-3 fats, which have been linked to heart and brain health.

Per 2 ounces: 140 calories, 12 g protein, 1 g carbs, 9 g fat, 1.5 g saturated fat, 0 g fiber, 260 mg sodium

Chobani Simply 100 Peach Greek Yogurt

This dairy delight uses monkfruit extract and peach for a fresh, not overly saccharine, flavor.

Per container: 100 calories, 12 g protein, 14 g carbs, 0 g fat, 0 g saturated fat, 5 g fiber, 65 mg sodium

Foods for a Fitter You!

Eating well helps you function at your peak, mentally and physically, and these foods are full of nutrients that help your body bounce back from the biological effects of stress. What better way to spoil yourself?

Dark Chocolate

This go-to mood booster has more polyphenols than some fruit juices and has been known to lower blood pressure. A 1-ounce square is the perfect portion.

Papaya

With vitamins A, C, and E, this tropical fruit is good for your skin, eyes, heart, and immune system. Try it fresh or, in small amounts, dried, to satisfy a sweet tooth.

Rosemary

Whether used topically or to season foods, the fragrant oil stimulates circulation and acts as an anti-irritant. Plus, this herb is a proven memory booster.

Flaxseed

Ground flax (easier to digest than whole seeds) is a dynamite source of lignans, plant estrogens that may soothe monthly mood swings and help prevent overeating.

Orange

This segmented citrus fruit is a powerhouse of vitamin C, an antioxidant that has been shown to help people recover more quickly from stress.

Celery

Crunching a stalk is stress-busting in itself, but celery also contains a chemical that lowers the concentration of stress hormones in the blood, relaxing constricted vessels.

Good Food, Fast

Thanks to these healthy picks and tips, you can head to the drive-thru without guilt weighing you down. These on-the-run meals won't break the calorie bank.

Breakfast

McDonald's Fruit 'n Yogurt Parfait

Low-fat dairy (like this vanilla yogurt) could help you shed pounds.

150 calories, 4 g protein, 30 g carbs, 2 g fat, 1 g saturated fat, 1 g fiber, 70 mg sodium

Dunkin' Donuts Ham & Egg Wake-Up Wrap

Load up on protein in the morning—it can help get your fat-burning engines running, stat.

170 calories, 10 g protein, 14 g carbs, 8 g fat, 3.5 g saturated fat, 1 g fiber, 560 mg sodium

Jamba Juice Make It Light! Banana Berry Smoothie

Jamba's new "Make It Light!" option means you get fresh, fruity flavors with up to one-third less sugar (and calories).

Small size: 170 calories, 5 g protein, 39 g carbs, 0 g fat, 0 g saturated fat, 3 g fiber, 125 mg sodium

SLIM-BODY EATS

Aiming for food quality rather than quantity may be your best bet if you're trying to drop pounds, reports a Harvard School of Public Health study. Researchers found a direct link between eating specific foods and beverages and weight gain or loss.

TOP FOODS FOR WEIGHT LOSS	TOP FOODS FOR WEIGHT GAIN
Yogurt	Potato chips
Nuts	Potatoes
Fruit	Sugar-sweetened beverages
Whole grains	Unprocessed red meats
Vegetables	Processed meats

Lunch/Dinner

Panera Power Steak Lettuce Wraps

In addition to its well-known list of deli eats, Panera Bread has a secret weapon: its hidden menu—your cashier will know what you're talking about—which includes six light and nutritious "Power" meals (from these wraps to salads to even egg-based breakfasts).

210 calories, 24 g protein, 7 g carbs, 10 g fat, 3.5 g saturated fat, 2 g fiber, 240 mg sodium

Wendy's Rich & Meaty Chili

Warm, satisfying, and bound to keep you full till dinner.

Large size: 270 calories, 19 g protein, 31 g carbs, 8 g fat, 3 g saturated fat, 7 g fiber, 1,180 mg sodium,

Subway Veggie Delite Salad with Honey Mustard Dressing and Poblano Corn Chowder

A meat-free lunch that doesn't skimp on protein and fiber.

260 calories, 8 g protein, 40 g carbs, 9 g fat, 4 g saturated fat, 6 g fiber, 880 mg sodium

---

SO WHAT'S IN A HEALTHY DINNER?

In a perfect world, every restaurant meal would meet our nutrition-ists' guidelines: Half the plate would be covered with vegetables, a quarter with lean protein (about 4 ounces of beef, chicken, or fish), and a quarter with a complex carbohydrate such as brown rice or sweet potatoes. When it comes to calories, for a woman on a typical 1,800-calorie daily diet, "I would recommend a 600-calorie dinner," says Tara Gidus, RD, a dietitian in Orlando, Florida. "And try to stay below 650 milligrams of sodium and 20 grams of fat." Many of the meals included here meet these criteria—but for those that don't, we show you how to alter them so they do.

Quiznos Turkey Lite Sub with Pasta Salad

Stick to the small sub size to keep sodium in check.

Small size: 470 calories, 24 g protein, 69 g carbs, 12 g fat, 2 g saturated fat, 7 g fiber, 1,230 mg sodium

Chipotle Burrito Bowl with Carnitas, Black Beans, and Tomatillo Salsa

Skip the rice, even brown: It sends the cals sky-high.

360 calories, 34 g protein, 26 g carbs, 14 g fat, 6 g saturated fat, 13 g fiber, 1,010 mg sodium

Have a Cow

A burger eaten in your car might never be as nutritious as a home-grilled one. But by making savvy choices or requesting mini tweaks when you order, you can steer your health in the right direction, says Lindsay Lawes, RD, a nutritionist in Boulder, Colorado.

1. Order the Happy Meal

You might feel silly using the word junior or kiddie, but kids' menu options often have half the calories of their grown-up equivalents. "Those portions may look skimpy," says Teresa Wagner, RD, a nutritionist in Dallas. "But they're often a lot closer to the amount you, as an adult, should be eating."

2. Hold the Bread

Carb-loaded white wraps, bread, and buns can pack plenty of calories and sodium while adding little flavor to your meal—which is why you can skip them altogether. Ask for a bunless burger (In-N-Out calls it Protein Style), a soup sans the bread bowl, or a burrito minus the tortilla. This trade-out can save you up to 300 calories.

3. Go Easy on the Sauce

It's old news that drizzling on dressing or sauce yourself instead of leaving it to heavy-handed cooks can shave off at least 100 calories. But even innocent-sounding sauces, like barbecue and teriyaki, can contain tons of hidden sugar (and calories). "Order your food as plain as you can," says Lawes, "then accent it yourself."

Week 7

YOUR WEEK AT A GLANCE

DAY	WORKOUT	MINUTES
1	Strength Training Workout 1 + After-Dinner Walk	20 + 30
2	After-Dinner Walk	30
3	After-Dinner Walk	30
4	Strength Training Workout 2 + After-Dinner Walk	20 + 30
5	After-Dinner Walk	30
6	After-Dinner Walk	30
7	After-Dinner Walk	30

What You'll Do This Week

EXERCISE

Day 1: Perform the 15-15-15 style, followed by 8 to 12 regular reps of each exercise.

Day 4: Perform the 15-15-15 style, followed by 8 to 12 regular reps of each exercise.

NUTRITION

Keep your caloric intake at 1,000 calories per day.

Belly Toning Tip

THE CASE FOR CREAM CHEESE Cutting back on the amount of dairy you eat can signal your body to make more fat cells, according to a study in the *American Journal of Clinical Nutrition*. When you don't have enough calcium in your body, it tries to hold on to what's there. This triggers the release of a compound called calcitriol, which increases the production of fat cells. If you want fewer fat cells, eating extra calcium suppresses calcitriol, which breaks down fat and makes your fat cells leaner and your tummy flatter. So enjoy the moo juice, yogurt, or a smear of cream cheese on your bagel. Because dairy does tend to be high in calories, keep your portions small or stick to low-fat varieties. (The USDA recommends that women get 3 cups of low-fat dairy a day.)

EXCUSE-PROOF YOUR WEEK

Staying focused during a workout will improve your performance and amp your results. But, when boredom or fatigue strikes during a workout, you might try to distract yourself by flicking on the TV or chatting up your treadmill neighbor. But tuning in—instead of checking out—may be the smarter tactic.

Experts say intention setting can be a powerful tool in any fitness discipline, not just yoga. "It zeros in on something you can connect to emotionally, and, unlike a long-term goal, you can make good on an intention in a single session, which is very satisfying," says celeb trainer Brett Hoebel. In other words, you can't, for example, lose 10 pounds during a 45-minute run, but you can feel happier or calmer by the end.

So set an intention (think "be strong" or "boost energy"—it can be different every time you exercise), then follow these tips to stay centered on it.

EXERCISE LOG

DATE:_____

Strength Training Workouts

Do $1\frac{1}{2}$ slow reps of each move below in 15-second, 15-second, 15-second negative-accentuated style, followed immediately by 8 to 12 regular-speed reps that progressively become more demanding.

MOVE	WORKOUT 1	WORKOUT 2
	DAY/DATE:	DAY/DATE:
Forward Crunch	Reps: 8 to 12	Reps: 8 to 12
Oblique Crunch (right and left)	R: Reps: 8 to 12 L: Reps: 8 to 12	R: Reps: 8 to 12 L: Reps: 8 to 12
V-Crunch	Reps: 8 to 12	Reps: 8 to 12
Pushup	Reps: 8 to 12	Reps: 8 to 12
Body Weight Squat	Reps: 8 to 12	Reps: 8 to 12

After-Dinner Walking Log

M:_____ TU:_____ W:_____ TH:_____ F:_____ SA: _____ SU:_____

SLEEP LOG

DATE:_____

DAY	BEDTIME	WAKING TIME	SLEEP QUALITY	NOTES
Monday				
Tuesday				
Wednesday				
Thursday				
Friday				
Saturday				
Sunday				

See the Light

Within 5 minutes of waking, try to expose yourself to up to 30 minutes of sunlight to give your brain the "It's morning!" signal, says Clete Kushida, MD, PhD, medical director of the Stanford Sleep Medicine Center. Then, continue to spend time in sunny spaces: A recent study found office workers who scored natural light during the day got an average of 46 more minutes of sleep per night than daylight-deprived coworkers.

FOOD LOG

DATE:_____

	FOOD	TIME	CALORIES	NOTES
Breakfast *(300 calories)*				
Lunch *(300 calories)*				
Snack *(50 calories)*				
Dinner *(300 calories)*				
Snack *(50 calories)*				

WATER LOG: ◯ ◯ ◯ ◯   1 Gallon or four 32-ounce tumblers

FOOD LOG

DATE:_____

	FOOD	TIME	CALORIES	NOTES
Breakfast *(300 calories)*				
Lunch *(300 calories)*				
Snack *(50 calories)*				
Dinner *(300 calories)*				
Snack *(50 calories)*				

WATER LOG: ◯ ◯ ◯ ◯   1 Gallon or four 32-ounce tumblers

FOOD LOG

DATE:_____

	FOOD	TIME	CALORIES	NOTES
Breakfast *(300 calories)*				
Lunch *(300 calories)*				
Snack *(50 calories)*				
Dinner *(300 calories)*				
Snack *(50 calories)*				

WATER LOG: ◯ ◯ ◯ ◯   1 Gallon or four 32-ounce tumblers

FOOD LOG

DATE:_____

	FOOD	TIME	CALORIES	NOTES
Breakfast (300 calories)				
Lunch (300 calories)				
Snack (50 calories)				
Dinner (300 calories)				
Snack (50 calories)				

WATER LOG: ◯ ◯ ◯ ◯   1 Gallon or four 32-ounce tumblers

FOOD LOG

DATE:_____

	FOOD	TIME	CALORIES	NOTES
Breakfast (300 calories)				
Lunch (300 calories)				
Snack (50 calories)				
Dinner (300 calories)				
Snack (50 calories)				

WATER LOG: ◯ ◯ ◯ ◯   1 Gallon or four 32-ounce tumblers

FOOD LOG

DATE:_____

	FOOD	TIME	CALORIES	NOTES
Breakfast (300 calories)				
Lunch (300 calories)				
Snack (50 calories)				
Dinner (300 calories)				
Snack (50 calories)				

WATER LOG: ◯ ◯ ◯ ◯   1 Gallon or four 32-ounce tumblers

FOOD LOG

DATE:_____

	FOOD	TIME	CALORIES	NOTES
Breakfast *(300 calories)*				
Lunch *(300 calories)*				
Snack *(50 calories)*				
Dinner *(300 calories)*				
Snack *(50 calories)*				

WATER LOG: ◯ ◯ ◯ ◯   1 Gallon or four 32-ounce tumblers

MEASUREMENTS

Body Weight:_____   Body Fat Percentage:_____

MEASUREMENTS

Waist:_____   Left Thigh:_____
(2" above navel)   *(just below the buttocks crease)*

Waist:_____   Right Thigh:_____
(at navel)   *(just below the buttocks crease)*

Waist:_____   Left Upper Arm:_____
(2" below navel)   *(hanging in middle)*

Hips:_____   Right Upper Arm:_____
(largest protrusion)   *(hanging in middle)*

ADDITIONAL NOTES: _____

_____

_____

_____

_____

_____

_____

_____

_____

_____

_____

_____

YOUR WEEK AT A GLANCE

DAY	WORKOUT	MINUTES
1	Strength Training Workout 1 + After-Dinner Walk	20 + 30
2	After-Dinner Walk	30
3	After-Dinner Walk	30
4	Strength Training Workout 2 + After-Dinner Walk	20 + 30
5	After-Dinner Walk	30
6	After-Dinner Walk	30
7	After-Dinner Walk	30

What You'll Do This Week

EXERCISE

Day 1: Perform the 15-15-15 style, followed by 8 to 12 regular reps of each exercise.

Day 4: Perform the 15-15-15 style, followed by 8 to 12 regular reps of each exercise.

NUTRITION

Hold steady at 1,000 calories per day.

EXCUSE-PROOF YOUR WEEK

Give yourself a pep talk! Turbocharge your motivation and trigger your intention with the help of a mantra—a word or phrase you repeat to psych yourself up—that reflects the purpose of your workout.

Think mantras are hokey? Try an updated version: Think of a mantra like a hashtag: #strongbodystrongmind, #bestshapeofmylife, #fitfromwithin. Or, if you're aiming to reduce stress and anxiety, try #justbreathe as your mantra. Want to feel strong? Go with #mindovermuscle. Mentally repeat your mantra throughout your workout—especially during the really tough parts, or when you catch your mind wandering.

You don't have to post a tweet or update your Facebook status to channel the empowering message; simply reminiscing why you started your weight loss journey will help keep you moving. Besides being inspiring, a mantra mentally hardwires your brain to enjoy exercise by acting as a cue to connect a behavior (exercise) with a reward (the positive experience of achieving your intention), says Charles Duhigg, author of *The Power of Habit*.

Belly Toning Tip

MASSAGE IT OUT A post-workout Swedish massage isn't just an indulgence: Research shows that it boosts strength recovery by 60 percent. Massage reduces inflammation in the tissue and increases blood flow to the area, which is what speeds up recovery, says Stacy Sims, PhD, an exercise physiologist and nutrition scientist at the Stanford School of Medicine's Prevention Research Center in Palo Alto, California. But you don't need to see a therapist—DIY rubdowns provide the same benefits. Set aside 10 minutes before bed on days when you exercise intensely, says Dr. Sims. For the best result, use long, smooth strokes over the muscles worked, and use a foam roller or massage balls on hard-to-reach spots. If you find a knot, move slowly from the outside in, but keep the pressure light to make sure you don't agitate an already inflamed muscle. For acute soreness, apply a cold compress or ice pack for about 20 minutes to further decrease inflammation.

EXERCISE LOG

DATE:_____

Strength Training Workouts

Do $1^1/_2$ slow reps of each move below in 15-second, 15-second, 15-second negative-accentuated style, followed immediately by 8 to 12 regular-speed reps that progressively become more demanding.

MOVE	WORKOUT 1	WORKOUT 2
	DAY/DATE:	DAY/DATE:
Forward Crunch	Reps: 8 to 12	Reps: 8 to 12
Oblique Crunch (right and left)	R: Reps: 8 to 12 L: Reps: 8 to 12	R: Reps: 8 to 12 L: Reps: 8 to 12
V-Crunch	Reps: 8 to 12	Reps: 8 to 12
Pushup	Reps: 8 to 12	Reps: 8 to 12
Body Weight Squat	Reps: 8 to 12	Reps: 8 to 12

After-Dinner Walking Log

M:_____ TU:_____ W:_____ TH:_____ F:_____ SA: _____ SU:_____

SLEEP LOG

DATE:_____

DAY	BEDTIME	WAKING TIME	SLEEP QUALITY	NOTES
Monday				
Tuesday				
Wednesday				
Thursday				
Friday				
Saturday				
Sunday				

Play a Lullaby

Those struggling to catch sufficient z's might want to crank up the tunes. Well, sort of. Studies suggest that listening to soothing music can help you relax. To set the stage for sleep, try songs with a continuous rhythm of about 60 beats per minute (such as "Weightless" by Marconi Union), which sync up with your resting heart rate, according to Lyz Cooper, founder of The British Academy of Sound Therapy.

FOOD LOG

DATE:_____

	FOOD	TIME	CALORIES	NOTES
Breakfast *(300 calories)*				
Lunch *(300 calories)*				
Snack *(50 calories)*				
Dinner *(300 calories)*				
Snack *(50 calories)*				

WATER LOG: ◯ ◯ ◯ ◯   1 Gallon or four 32-ounce tumblers

FOOD LOG

DATE:_____

	FOOD	TIME	CALORIES	NOTES
Breakfast *(300 calories)*				
Lunch *(300 calories)*				
Snack *(50 calories)*				
Dinner *(300 calories)*				
Snack *(50 calories)*				

WATER LOG: ◯ ◯ ◯ ◯   1 Gallon or four 32-ounce tumblers

FOOD LOG

DATE:_____

	FOOD	TIME	CALORIES	NOTES
Breakfast *(300 calories)*				
Lunch *(300 calories)*				
Snack *(50 calories)*				
Dinner *(300 calories)*				
Snack *(50 calories)*				

WATER LOG: ○ ○ ○ ○ 1 Gallon or four 32-ounce tumblers

FOOD LOG

DATE:_____

	FOOD	TIME	CALORIES	NOTES
Breakfast *(300 calories)*				
Lunch *(300 calories)*				
Snack *(50 calories)*				
Dinner *(300 calories)*				
Snack *(50 calories)*				

WATER LOG: ◯ ◯ ◯ ◯   1 Gallon or four 32-ounce tumblers

FOOD LOG

DATE:_____

	FOOD	TIME	CALORIES	NOTES
Breakfast (300 calories)				
Lunch (300 calories)				
Snack (50 calories)				
Dinner (300 calories)				
Snack (50 calories)				

WATER LOG: ◯ ◯ ◯ ◯   1 Gallon or four 32-ounce tumblers

FOOD LOG

DATE:_____

	FOOD	TIME	CALORIES	NOTES
Breakfast *(300 calories)*				
Lunch *(300 calories)*				
Snack *(50 calories)*				
Dinner *(300 calories)*				
Snack *(50 calories)*				

WATER LOG: ◯ ◯ ◯ ◯   1 Gallon or four 32-ounce tumblers

FOOD LOG

DATE:_____

	FOOD	TIME	CALORIES	NOTES
Breakfast (300 calories)				
Lunch (300 calories)				
Snack (50 calories)				
Dinner (300 calories)				
Snack (50 calories)				

WATER LOG: ◯ ◯ ◯ ◯   1 Gallon or four 32-ounce tumblers

MEASUREMENTS

Body Weight:_____   Body Fat Percentage:_____

MEASUREMENTS

Waist:_____
(2" above navel)

Waist:_____
(at navel)

Waist:_____
(2" below navel)

Hips:_____
(largest protrusion)

Left Thigh:_____
(just below the buttocks crease)

Right Thigh:_____
(just below the buttocks crease)

Left Upper Arm:_____
(hanging in middle)

Right Upper Arm:_____
(hanging in middle)

ADDITIONAL NOTES: _____

_____

_____

_____

_____

_____

_____

_____

_____

_____

_____

_____

Week 9

YOUR WEEK AT A GLANCE

DAY	WORKOUT	MINUTES
1	Strength Training Workout 1 + After-Dinner Walk	20 + 30
2	After-Dinner Walk	30
3	After-Dinner Walk	30
4	Strength Training Workout 2 + After Dinner Walk	20 + 30
5	After-Dinner Walk	30
6	After-Dinner Walk	30
7	After-Dinner Walk	30

What You'll Do This Week

EXERCISE

Day 1: You'll be reintroducing the dumbbell curl to your workouts this week. Perform the 15-15-15 style, followed by 8 to 12 regular reps of each exercise.

Day 4: Increase the weight of your dumbbells 5 percent, perform the 15-15-15 style, followed by 8 to 12 regular reps of each exercise.

NUTRITION

Weigh yourself at least three times a week. While 1 or 2 pounds of variation is normal, an increase of 4 or 5 pounds is a sign it's time to tweak your calories, especially in the last few week of the program.

EXCUSE-PROOF YOUR WEEK

Sync your workout. Plugging in your iPod during a workout might seem like an odd way to increase your focus—after all, plenty of us use music to mentally check out—but research shows that listening to certain types of tunes can actually help you keep your mind squarely on what you're doing and keep you motivated to complete a task.

Create a playlist that uses words or themes that speak to the intention that you've picked for that day's workout—and crank up the volume when you feel like you're starting to flag. If your intention is "go faster," add Eminem's "'Till I Collapse," Kanye West's "Stronger," and Florence + the Machine's "Dog Days Are Over" to your list. Looking to gain more happiness by the end of your workout? Crank up "I Gotta Feeling" by the Black Eyed Peas, "Beautiful Day" by U2, and "I Love It" by Icona Pop. Choose as many songs as you need for your playlist to be effective and feed your intention.

A study in the journal *The Sport Psychologist* found that tennis players recorded faster reaction times on the court when they listened to songs with an emotionally charged message (e.g., "Eye of the Tiger" from *Rocky III*), as compared to music with a booty-shaking rhythm but not much in the way of motivation (say, Beyonce's "Single Ladies"). "Songs with strong lyrical affirmations can give you a significant physical and mental boost when the going gets tough," says study author Costas Karageorghis, PhD, author of *Inside Sport Psychology*.

Belly Toning Tip

TURN BACK THE CLOCK Plan workouts when you have the fewest conflicts, which for most people is first thing in the a.m. Not an early riser? Inch your alarm back a little every few days; it will gradually reset your body's clock, so you'll have more energy, says Ken Baum, author of *The Mental Edge*. If you love (or need) to hit the gym at night, get changed before you leave work. That initial step will help you follow through.

Strength Training Workouts

Do 1 ½ slow reps of each move below in 15-second, 15-second, 15-second negative-accentuated style, followed immediately by 8 to 12 regular-speed reps that progressively become more demanding.

MOVE	WORKOUT 1	WORKOUT 2
	DAY/DATE:	DAY/DATE:
Forward Crunch	Reps: 8 to 12	Reps: 8 to 12
Oblique Crunch (right and left)	**R:** Reps: 8 to 12 **L:** Reps: 8 to 12	**R:** Reps: 8 to 12 **L:** Reps: 8 to 12
V-Crunch	Reps: 8 to 12	Reps: 8 to 12
Pushup	Reps: 8 to 12	Reps: 8 to 12
Body Weight Squat	Reps: 8 to 12	Reps: 8 to 12
Dumbbell Curl	Reps: 8 to 12	Reps: 8 to 12

After-Dinner Walking Log

M:_____ TU:_____ W:_____ TH:_____ F:_____ SA: _____ SU:_____

SLEEP LOG

DATE:_____

DAY	BEDTIME	WAKING TIME	SLEEP QUALITY	NOTES
Monday				
Tuesday				
Wednesday				
Thursday				
Friday				
Saturday				
Sunday				

Embrace Carbs at Dinner, Too

The insulin spike you get from eating fare such as brown rice, yams, or pasta may help you fall asleep faster, per research published in the journal *Cell*. Aim for 15 to 20 grams at your evening meal, about the amount in half a cup of quinoa or whole-grain spaghetti.

FOOD LOG

DATE:_____

	FOOD	TIME	CALORIES	NOTES
Breakfast *(300 calories)*				
Snack *(50 calories)*				
Lunch *(300 calories)*				
Snack *(150 calories)*				
Dinner *(300 calories)*				
Snack *(100 calories)*				

WATER LOG: ◯ ◯ ◯ ◯   1 Gallon or four 32-ounce tumblers

FOOD LOG

DATE:_____

	FOOD	TIME	CALORIES	NOTES
Breakfast *(300 calories)*				
Snack *(50 calories)*				
Lunch *(300 calories)*				
Snack *(150 calories)*				
Dinner *(300 calories)*				
Snack *(100 calories)*				

WATER LOG: ◯ ◯ ◯ ◯   1 Gallon or four 32-ounce tumblers

FOOD LOG

DATE:_____

	FOOD	TIME	CALORIES	NOTES
Breakfast *(300 calories)*				
Snack *(50 calories)*				
Lunch *(300 calories)*				
Snack *(150 calories)*				
Dinner *(300 calories)*				
Snack *(100 calories)*				

WATER LOG: ◯ ◯ ◯ ◯ 1 Gallon or four 32-ounce tumblers

FOOD LOG

DATE:_____

	FOOD	TIME	CALORIES	NOTES
Breakfast *(300 calories)*				
Snack *(50 calories)*				
Lunch *(300 calories)*				
Snack *(150 calories)*				
Dinner *(300 calories)*				
Snack *(100 calories)*				

WATER LOG: ◯ ◯ ◯ ◯ 1 Gallon or four 32-ounce tumblers

FOOD LOG

DATE:_____

	FOOD	TIME	CALORIES	NOTES
Breakfast *(300 calories)*				
Snack *(50 calories)*				
Lunch *(300 calories)*				
Snack *(150 calories)*				
Dinner *(300 calories)*				
Snack *(100 calories)*				

WATER LOG: ◯ ◯ ◯ ◯   1 Gallon or four 32-ounce tumblers

FOOD LOG

DATE:_____

	FOOD	TIME	CALORIES	NOTES
Breakfast *(300 calories)*				
Snack *(50 calories)*				
Lunch *(300 calories)*				
Snack *(150 calories)*				
Dinner *(300 calories)*				
Snack *(100 calories)*				

WATER LOG: ◯ ◯ ◯ ◯   1 Gallon or four 32-ounce tumblers

FOOD LOG

DATE:_____

	FOOD	TIME	CALORIES	NOTES
Breakfast *(300 calories)*				
Snack *(50 calories)*				
Lunch *(300 calories)*				
Snack *(150 calories)*				
Dinner *(300 calories)*				
Snack *(100 calories)*				

WATER LOG: ◯ ◯ ◯ ◯   1 Gallon or four 32-ounce tumblers

MEASUREMENTS

DATE:_____

Body Weight:_____   Body Fat Percentage:_____

MEASUREMENTS

Waist:_____
(2" above navel)

Left Thigh:_____
(just below the buttocks crease)

Waist:_____
(at navel)

Right Thigh:_____
(just below the buttocks crease)

Waist:_____
(2" below navel)

Left Upper Arm:_____
(hanging in middle)

Hips:_____
(largest protrusion)

Right Upper Arm:_____
(hanging in middle)

ADDITIONAL NOTES: _____

_____

_____

_____

_____

_____

_____

_____

_____

_____

_____

_____

YOUR WEEK AT A GLANCE

DAY	WORKOUT	MINUTES
1	Strength Training Workout 1 + After-Dinner Walk	20 + 30
2	After-Dinner Walk	30
3	After-Dinner Walk	30
4	Strength Training Workout 2 + After-Dinner Walk	20 + 30
5	After-Dinner Walk	30
6	After-Dinner Walk	30
7	After-Dinner Walk	30

What You'll Do This Week

EXERCISE

Day 1: Perform the 15-15-15 style, followed by 8 to 12 regular reps of each exercise.

Day 4: Perform the 15-15-15 style, followed by 8 to 12 regular reps of each exercise.

NUTRITION

Remember to keep your meals in the 300-calorie range and snacks between 50 and 100 calories. If you're having trouble with portion control, use frozen entrees to reacquaint yourself with what 50:25:25 should look like on your plate.

Belly Toning Tip

TAKE IT OUTSIDE Join the new "green exercise movement." Move your workout outside and you'll soak up the beauty and the benefits of being in nature. Studies show that as little as 5 minutes of walking in a natural setting can increase your self-esteem, boost your mood, and slash high blood pressure. Not only that, but new research says that people who are active outdoors exercise longer than those who work out inside only. So lace up your shoes and head for the park or hit the trail. Mother Nature will reward you.

EXCUSE-PROOF YOUR WEEK

You already know staying hydrated maintains and supports building lean muscle mass to keep your metabolism humming, and that H_2O increases calorie burn when it's super frosty. But, if you're sill having trouble guzzling a whole gallon of ice water, consider this: Making your drink of choice green or oolong tea can also give your metabolism an added boost, according to Japanese researchers.

So, want to painlessly burn off a few extra calories and add a little variety to your brews? Sip this.

Iced Lemon and Ginger Green Tea

Serves 6 (enough for a glass a day!)

1. Combine 10 green or oolong tea bags, 2" piece peeled fresh ginger cut into thin slices, 3 large mint sprigs, and 1 sliced small lemon in heatproof 2 quart pitcher.

2. Bring 4 cups water to a boil in saucepan and pour into pitcher.

3. Stir once and let tea bags steep 6 minutes.

4. Remove and discard tea bags and mint sprigs.

5. Add a touch of honey to tea, if desired.

6. Let cool 20 minutes.

7. Add enough ice and cold water to make 6 cups.

8. Serve over ice in glasses with fresh mint sprigs and lemon slices.

EXERCISE LOG

DATE:_____

Strength Training Workouts

Do 1½ slow reps of each move below in 15-second, 15-second, 15-second negative-accentuated style, followed immediately by 8 to 12 regular-speed reps that progressively become more demanding.

MOVE	WORKOUT 1	WORKOUT 2
	DAY/DATE:	DAY/DATE:
Forward Crunch	Reps: 8 to 12	Reps: 8 to 12
Oblique Crunch (right and left)	R: Reps: 8 to 12 L: Reps: 8 to 12	R: Reps: 8 to 12 L: Reps: 8 to 12
V-Crunch	Reps: 8 to 12	Reps: 8 to 12
Pushup	Reps: 8 to 12	Reps: 8 to 12
Body Weight Squat	Reps: 8 to 12	Reps: 8 to 12
Dumbbell Curl	Reps: 8 to 12	Reps: 8 to 12

After-Dinner Walking Log

M:_____ TU:_____ W:_____ TH:_____ F:_____ SA: _____ SU:_____

SLEEP LOG

DATE:_____

DAY	BEDTIME	WAKING TIME	SLEEP QUALITY	NOTES
Monday				
Tuesday				
Wednesday				
Thursday				
Friday				
Saturday				
Sunday				

Don't Stew

To keep from lying awake itemizing all of your worries, grab a pen and paper a few hours before bed each night and jot down your to-dos or qualms. "When you address what's bothering you, you're actually mentally checking it off a list," says Clete Kushida, MD, PhD, medical director of the Stanford Sleep Medicine Center.

FOOD LOG

DATE:_____

	FOOD	TIME	CALORIES	NOTES
Breakfast *(300 calories)*				
Snack *(50 calories)*				
Lunch *(300 calories)*				
Snack *(150 calories)*				
Dinner *(300 calories)*				
Snack *(100 calories)*				

WATER LOG: ◯ ◯ ◯ ◯   1 Gallon or four 32-ounce tumblers

FOOD LOG

DATE:_____

	FOOD	TIME	CALORIES	NOTES
Breakfast *(300 calories)*				
Snack *(50 calories)*				
Lunch *(300 calories)*				
Snack *(150 calories)*				
Dinner *(300 calories)*				
Snack *(100 calories)*				

WATER LOG: ○ ○ ○ ○   1 Gallon or four 32-ounce tumblers

FOOD LOG

DATE:_____

	FOOD	TIME	CALORIES	NOTES
Breakfast *(300 calories)*				
Snack *(50 calories)*				
Lunch *(300 calories)*				
Snack *(150 calories)*				
Dinner *(300 calories)*				
Snack *(100 calories)*				

WATER LOG: ◯ ◯ ◯ ◯   1 Gallon or four 32-ounce tumblers

FOOD LOG

DATE:_____

	FOOD	TIME	CALORIES	NOTES
Breakfast (300 calories)				
Snack (50 calories)				
Lunch (300 calories)				
Snack (150 calories)				
Dinner (300 calories)				
Snack (100 calories)				

WATER LOG: ◯ ◯ ◯ ◯ 1 Gallon or four 32-ounce tumblers

FOOD LOG

DATE:_____

	FOOD	TIME	CALORIES	NOTES
Breakfast (300 calories)				
Snack (50 calories)				
Lunch (300 calories)				
Snack (150 calories)				
Dinner (300 calories)				
Snack (100 calories)				

WATER LOG: ◯ ◯ ◯ ◯   1 Gallon or four 32-ounce tumblers

FOOD LOG

DATE:_____

	FOOD	TIME	CALORIES	NOTES
Breakfast (300 calories)				
Snack (50 calories)				
Lunch (300 calories)				
Snack (150 calories)				
Dinner (300 calories)				
Snack (100 calories)				

WATER LOG: ◯ ◯ ◯ ◯   1 Gallon or four 32-ounce tumblers

FOOD LOG

DATE:_____

	FOOD	TIME	CALORIES	NOTES
Breakfast (300 calories)				
Snack (50 calories)				
Lunch (300 calories)				
Snack (150 calories)				
Dinner (300 calories)				
Snack (100 calories)				

WATER LOG: ◯ ◯ ◯ ◯   1 Gallon or four 32-ounce tumblers

MEASUREMENTS

Body Weight:_____   Body Fat Percentage:_____

MEASUREMENTS

Waist:_____
(2" above navel)

Waist:_____
(at navel)

Waist:_____
(2" below navel)

Hips:_____
(largest protrusion)

Left Thigh:_____
(just below the buttocks crease)

Right Thigh:_____
(just below the buttocks crease)

Left Upper Arm:_____
(hanging in middle)

Right Upper Arm:_____
(hanging in middle)

ADDITIONAL NOTES: _____

_____

_____

_____

_____

_____

_____

_____

_____

_____

_____

Week 11

YOUR WEEK AT A GLANCE

DAY	WORKOUT	MINUTES
1	Strength Training Workout 1 + After-Dinner Walk	20 + 30
2	After-Dinner Walk	30
3	After-Dinner Walk	30
4	Strength Training Workout 2 + After-Dinner Walk	20 + 30
5	After-Dinner Walk	30
6	After-Dinner Walk	30
7	After-Dinner Walk	30

What You'll Do This Week

EXERCISE

Day 1: This week, you'll add the dumbbell overhead press to your workouts once again. Perform the 15-15-15 style, followed by 8 to 12 regular reps for each exercise.

Day 4: Perform the 15-15-15 style, followed by 8 to 12 regular reps for each exercise.

NUTRITION

Finish these last 2 weeks strong, strictly following your 1,100 calorie plan. Remember: Each meal should be balanced with 50 percent carbs, 25 percent fat, and 25 percent protein.

EXCUSE-PROOF YOUR WEEK

It's Week 11 and you've almost finished your SECOND cycle of the program! Pat yourself on the back, but note, this week and next can be especially tough. The upside: You're used to the workouts. The downside? Your routine is becoming more mundane as you close in on the final week. Make some "me" time to savor your success and bounce out of the boredom funk.

Women tend to save rewards for distant, huge goals, like a 20-pound weight loss or three lost dress sizes, says Howard Rankin, PhD, psychological advisor to the national Take Off Pounds Sensibly (TOPS) organization in Hilton Head, South Carolina.

Rather than make goals destination-oriented, make them behavior-oriented. Set a goal to stick to your workouts and calories strictly this week—skipping just one workout can raise your odds of missing another the following week by 61 percent, according to UK research. When Sunday rolls around, give yourself a nonfood reward, like a glossy magazine or new nail polish—little indulgences you wouldn't ordinarily give yourself.

Belly Toning Tip

A 10-SECOND TRICK TO NEVER EVER GAIN WEIGHT About to order that scone with your latte? Do a little math on how much time it will take to burn off the treat. A study shows that considering the exercise equivalent rather than just the calorie count helps us make the choice we don't regret.

TREAT	CALORIES	MINUTES WALKING
Au Bon Pain Classic Oatmeal Raisin Cookie	290	72
Starbucks Double Chocolate Chunk Brownie	380	94
Dunkin' Donuts Blueberry Muffin	460	114
Panera Bread Cinnamon Roll	630	155
Cheesecake Factory Vanilla Bean Cheesecake	870	215

EXERCISE LOG

DATE:_____

Strength Training Workouts

Do 1½ slow reps of each move below in 15-second, 15-second, 15-second negative-accentuated style, followed immediately by 8 to 12 regular-speed reps that progressively become more demanding.

MOVE	WORKOUT 1	WORKOUT 2
	DAY/DATE:	DAY/DATE:
Forward Crunch	Reps: 8 to 12	Reps: 8 to 12
Oblique Crunch (right and left)	R: Reps: 8 to 12 L: Reps: 8 to 12	R: Reps: 8 to 12 L: Reps: 8 to 12
V-Crunch	Reps: 8 to 12	Reps: 8 to 12
Pushup	Reps: 8 to 12	Reps: 8 to 12
Body Weight Squat	Reps: 8 to 12	Reps: 8 to 12
Dumbbell Curl	Reps: 8 to 12	Reps: 8 to 12
Dumbbell Overhead Press	Reps: 8 to 12	Reps: 8 to 12

After-Dinner Walking Log

M:_____ TU:_____ W:_____ TH:_____ F:_____ SA: _____ SU:_____

SLEEP LOG

DATE:_____

DAY	BEDTIME	WAKING TIME	SLEEP QUALITY	NOTES
Monday				
Tuesday				
Wednesday				
Thursday				
Friday				
Saturday				
Sunday				

Exercise in the A.M.

Not only can early-bird workouts squash cortisol levels for up to 12 hours, but new research shows that people who do 30 minutes of moderate cardio in the morning fall asleep quicker, snooze for longer, and spend up to 75 percent more time in deep sleep than those who sweat later in the day.

Yoga also works, at any hour. The practice is ace at zapping stress, and studies show that dedicated yogis have better overall sleep quality, says Sat Bir Singh Khalsa, PhD, an assistant professor of Medicine at Harvard Medical School.

FOOD LOG

DATE:_____

	FOOD	TIME	CALORIES	NOTES
Breakfast *(300 calories)*				
Snack *(50 calories)*				
Lunch *(300 calories)*				
Snack *(50 calories)*				
Dinner *(300 calories)*				
Snack *(100 calories)*				

WATER LOG: ◯ ◯ ◯ ◯   1 Gallon or four 32-ounce tumblers

FOOD LOG

DATE:_____

	FOOD	TIME	CALORIES	NOTES
Breakfast *(300 calories)*				
Snack *(50 calories)*				
Lunch *(300 calories)*				
Snack *(50 calories)*				
Dinner *(300 calories)*				
Snack *(100 calories)*				

WATER LOG: ◯ ◯ ◯ ◯   1 Gallon or four 32-ounce tumblers

FOOD LOG

DATE:_____

	FOOD	TIME	CALORIES	NOTES
Breakfast *(300 calories)*				
Snack *(50 calories)*				
Lunch *(300 calories)*				
Snack *(50 calories)*				
Dinner *(300 calories)*				
Snack *(100 calories)*				

WATER LOG: ◯ ◯ ◯ ◯   1 Gallon or four 32-ounce tumblers

FOOD LOG

DATE:_____

	FOOD	TIME	CALORIES	NOTES
Breakfast *(300 calories)*				
Snack *(50 calories)*				
Lunch *(300 calories)*				
Snack *(50 calories)*				
Dinner *(300 calories)*				
Snack *(100 calories)*				

WATER LOG: ◯ ◯ ◯ ◯   1 Gallon or four 32-ounce tumblers

FOOD LOG

DATE:_____

	FOOD	TIME	CALORIES	NOTES
Breakfast (300 calories)				
Snack (50 calories)				
Lunch (300 calories)				
Snack (50 calories)				
Dinner (300 calories)				
Snack (100 calories)				

WATER LOG: ◯ ◯ ◯ ◯   1 Gallon or four 32-ounce tumblers

FOOD LOG

DATE:_____

	FOOD	TIME	CALORIES	NOTES
Breakfast *(300 calories)*				
Snack *(50 calories)*				
Lunch *(300 calories)*				
Snack *(50 calories)*				
Dinner *(300 calories)*				
Snack *(100 calories)*				

WATER LOG: ◯ ◯ ◯ ◯   1 Gallon or four 32-ounce tumblers

FOOD LOG

DATE:_____

	FOOD	TIME	CALORIES	NOTES
Breakfast *(300 calories)*				
Snack *(50 calories)*				
Lunch *(300 calories)*				
Snack *(50 calories)*				
Dinner *(300 calories)*				
Snack *(100 calories)*				

WATER LOG: ◯ ◯ ◯ ◯   1 Gallon or four 32-ounce tumblers

MEASUREMENTS

DATE:_____

Body Weight:_____   Body Fat Percentage:_____

MEASUREMENTS

Waist:_____
(2" above navel)

Waist:_____
(at navel)

Waist:_____
(2" below navel)

Hips:_____
(largest protrusion)

Left Thigh:_____
(just below the buttocks crease)

Right Thigh:_____
(just below the buttocks crease)

Left Upper Arm:_____
(hanging in middle)

Right Upper Arm:_____
(hanging in middle)

ADDITIONAL NOTES: _____

_____

_____

_____

_____

_____

_____

_____

_____

_____

_____

_____

Week 12

YOUR WEEK AT A GLANCE

DAY	WORKOUT	MINUTES
1	Strength Training Workout 1 + After-Dinner Walk	20 + 30
2	After-Dinner Walk	30
3	After-Dinner Walk	30
4	Strength Training Workout 2 + After-Dinner Walk	20 + 30
5	After-Dinner Walk	30
6	After-Dinner Walk	30
7	After-Dinner Walk	30

What You'll Do This Week

EXERCISE

Day 1: Perform the 15-15-15 style, followed by 8 to 12 regular reps for each exercise.

Day 4: Perform the 15-15-15 style, followed by 8 to 12 regular reps for each exercise.

NUTRITION

It's your last week of cycle two! If you find your weight loss stalled, try varying your meal times to stoke your fat burn.

Belly Toning Tip

EVERY MINUTE COUNTS (REALLY!) One more reason to trash an all-or-nothing workout mentality: Walking just 20 minutes a day could add years to your life. After following more than 334,000 adults for 12 years, researchers found that, compared with inactive people, those who consistently logged at least 20 daily minutes of moderate exercise were more than 20 percent less likely to die prematurely than their more chair-bound counterparts.

EXCUSE-PROOF YOUR WEEK

It's your final week! Save the celebrations for the absolute last day and take time this week to focus on meeting your overall goal. Have you met it? Surpassed it? Fallen a step back?

Goals are key to keep you going when things start to stall. And just because you've done a fantastic job sticking to them the past 12 weeks, that doesn't mean you have to abandon the practice of making new (or short-term) goals after you've finished the program—epecially if you want to maintain your smokin' new bod.

So, this week, set aside 10 minutes to craft your post–Flat Belly Breakthrough goals. Use these five principles to get started.

GET SPECIFIC: Set out to just "be healthy" and you're selling yourself short. Vague goals give people too much leeway and can lower their motivation to push themselves. So be precise and say, for example, that you want to lower your body fat by 10 percent or be able to run a 10-K.

MAKE THEM MEASURABLE: You should be able to gauge and quantify your progress, both in the short-term and long-term. Set micro (weekly) and macro (monthly) goals to keep yourself on track.

ENSURE THEY'RE ATTAINABLE: If you can barely find 20 free minutes in your day, don't set yourself up for failure by saying you'll run for 50 minutes three days a week.

...AND REALISTIC: Even with the smartest plan and the strongest determination, your body can only handle so much. Sure, fast weight loss is possible, but if you drop more than about a pound and a half a week, you're most likely looking at muscle and water loss—not fat.

BE TIME SENSITIVE: Deadlines create a sense of urgency and make your goal a priority. Give yourself a year to drop 75 to 100 pounds, 4 to 6 months to train for a marathon (if you're a new runner), and two months to lose 10 percent to 12 percent of your body fat.

EXERCISE LOG

Strength Training Workouts

Do 1½ slow reps of each move below in 15-second, 15-second, 15-second negative-accentuated style, followed immediately by 8 to 12 regular-speed reps that progressively become more demanding.

MOVE	WORKOUT 1	WORKOUT 2
	DAY/DATE:	DAY/DATE:
Forward Crunch	Reps: 8 to 12	Reps: 8 to 12
Oblique Crunch (right and left)	R: Reps: 8 to 12 L: Reps: 8 to 12	R: Reps: 8 to 12 L: Reps: 8 to 12
V-Crunch	Reps: 8 to 12	Reps: 8 to 12
Pushup	Reps: 8 to 12	Reps: 8 to 12
Body Weight Squat	Reps: 8 to 12	Reps: 8 to 12
Dumbbell Curl	Reps: 8 to 12	Reps: 8 to 12
Dumbbell Overheard Press	Reps: 8 to 12	Reps: 8 to 12

After-Dinner Walking Log

M:_____ TU:_____ W:_____ TH:_____ F:_____ SA: _____ SU:_____

SLEEP LOG

DATE:_____

DAY	BEDTIME	WAKING TIME	SLEEP QUALITY	NOTES
Monday				
Tuesday				
Wednesday				
Thursday				
Friday				
Saturday				
Sunday				

Still Struggling to Sleep?

Strap on a monitor, or download an app for extra help. Sleep trackers use motion sensors to measure even your most subtle wake-ups throughout the night, plus how long and how well you snooze—all info you can use to get better subsequent shut-eye. Try out the super-affordable Sleep Cycle app (iTunes, Android), which works with smartphone technology to analyze your every dozing moment, then wakes you during your lightest sleep stage.

FOOD LOG

DATE:_____

	FOOD	TIME	CALORIES	NOTES
Breakfast (300 calories)				
Snack (50 calories)				
Lunch (300 calories)				
Snack (50 calories)				
Dinner (300 calories)				
Snack (100 calories)				

WATER LOG: ◯ ◯ ◯ ◯   1 Gallon or four 32-ounce tumblers

FOOD LOG

DATE:_____

	FOOD	TIME	CALORIES	NOTES
Breakfast (300 calories)				
Snack (50 calories)				
Lunch (300 calories)				
Snack (50 calories)				
Dinner (300 calories)				
Snack (100 calories)				

WATER LOG: ◯ ◯ ◯ ◯   1 Gallon or four 32-ounce tumblers

FOOD LOG

DATE:_____

	FOOD	TIME	CALORIES	NOTES
Breakfast *(300 calories)*				
Snack *(50 calories)*				
Lunch *(300 calories)*				
Snack *(50 calories)*				
Dinner *(300 calories)*				
Snack *(100 calories)*				

WATER LOG: ◯ ◯ ◯ ◯   1 Gallon or four 32-ounce tumblers

FOOD LOG

DATE:_____

	FOOD	TIME	CALORIES	NOTES
Breakfast *(300 calories)*				
Snack *(50 calories)*				
Lunch *(300 calories)*				
Snack *(50 calories)*				
Dinner *(300 calories)*				
Snack *(100 calories)*				

WATER LOG: ◯ ◯ ◯ ◯   1 Gallon or four 32-ounce tumblers

FOOD LOG

DATE:_____

	FOOD	TIME	CALORIES	NOTES
Breakfast (300 calories)				
Snack (50 calories)				
Lunch (300 calories)				
Snack (50 calories)				
Dinner (300 calories)				
Snack (100 calories)				

WATER LOG: ○ ○ ○ ○   1 Gallon or four 32-ounce tumblers

FOOD LOG

DATE:_____

	FOOD	TIME	CALORIES	NOTES
Breakfast *(300 calories)*				
Snack *(50 calories)*				
Lunch *(300 calories)*				
Snack *(50 calories)*				
Dinner *(300 calories)*				
Snack *(100 calories)*				

WATER LOG: ◯ ◯ ◯ ◯   1 Gallon or four 32-ounce tumblers

FOOD LOG

DATE:_____

	FOOD	TIME	CALORIES	NOTES
Breakfast *(300 calories)*				
Snack *(50 calories)*				
Lunch *(300 calories)*				
Snack *(50 calories)*				
Dinner *(300 calories)*				
Snack *(100 calories)*				

WATER LOG: ○ ○ ○ ○   1 Gallon or four 32-ounce tumblers

MEASUREMENTS

Body Weight:_____   Body Fat Percentage:_____

MEASUREMENTS

Waist:_____
(2" above navel)

Left Thigh:_____
(just below the buttocks crease)

Waist:_____
(at navel)

Right Thigh:_____
(just below the buttocks crease)

Waist:_____
(2" below navel)

Left Upper Arm:_____
(hanging in middle)

Hips:_____
(largest protrusion)

Right Upper Arm:_____
(hanging in middle)

ADDITIONAL NOTES: _____

_____

_____

_____

_____

_____

_____

_____

_____

_____

_____

_____

Lose Weight, Feel Great WALKING TIPS

Walking doesn't get the credit it deserves. The last time anyone made a big deal about walking was probably when you were 12 months old. But after that, the magic moment wore off and no one (including you) paid it much mind. Since it's such an integral part of our lives, most of us fail to see it as a vital component of good health that we can leverage for weight loss.

Research shows that with 30 minutes of moderate exercise daily, you will live longer—and enjoy your years much more—than someone who

MOVEMENT IS YOUR MUSE

Here's some old advice: Go for a walk to clear your head. New research from Stanford University confirms that moving forward is an effective strategy for freer thinking. Walkers had 60 percent more creative ideas than their seated peers, and they didn't even have to go outside (or break a sweat) to get results—a leisurely treadmill stroll facing a boring blank wall worked, too. Researchers think that walking might hog enough of our brainpower to let in ideas we'd normally filter out. No need for a treadmill desk, by the way; the creative edge lasts even after you stop ambling and sit.

just sits around all day. On the Flat Belly Breakthrough program you'll be hitting the road for 30 minutes after dinner for a stroll every day. And trust us, it's the easiest weight-loss plan ever—one that doesn't require making drastic changes to your diet—with the most lasting, overall health results. But, that's not to say it doesn't get, er, a little boring every once in a while.

That's where this section comes in handy. Here you'll find walking routines, tips, and advice that will motivate you to take a hike—literally—and equip you with what you need to blaze a happy trail—even if it's just around your block. Grab your sneaks, and let's go!

Your Body on Walking

Ridiculously simple, astonishingly powerful, scientifically proven by study after study: Sneaking in a few minutes a day can transform your health, body, and mind. Why are you still sitting?

Brain: Just 2 hours of walking a week can reduce your risk of stroke by 30 percent.

Memory: 40 minutes three times a week protects the brain region associated with planning and memory.

Mood: 30 minutes a day can reduce symptoms of depression by 36 percent.

Health: Logging 3,500 steps a day lowers your risk of diabetes by 29 percent.

Longevity: 75 minutes a week of brisk walking can add almost 2 years to your life.

Heart: 30 to 60 minutes most days of the week drastically lowers your risk of heart disease.

A GAIT WAY TO LIVE LONGER

Don't underestimate the power of a daily stroll. Walking can cut your risk of dying of brain cancer by about 40 percent, according to new research from the Lawrence Berkeley National Laboratory. The magic minimum needed to reap the benefit: 12 miles a week.

Bones: 4 hours a week can reduce the risk of hip fractures by up to 43 percent.

Weight: A daily 1-hour walk can cut your risk of obesity in half.

After-Dinner Walk? Chew On This.

Walk fast, eat slow. Before you head out for your Flat Belly Breakthrough stroll after dinner, take a minute to think about how quickly you ate. While a nice walk after dinner can help aid digestion, wolfing down your last meal of the day can cause the health benefits to dissipate faster than what was on your plate.

What's more, eating too fast can cause you to eat a lot more food than you really need. Why? It takes about 20 minutes for your brain and your belly to get on the same wavelength. If you're eating fast, chances are you'll wind up stuffed. Here's how to bypass your speed control.

USE YOUR FEET TO BEAT DIABETES

It's no secret that the number of Americans with type 2 diabetes, a chronic disease characterized by high blood sugar, is at epidemic levels. Right now, nearly 18 million Americans have been diagnosed with the disease, but another 7 million have it and don't know it, putting them at higher risk of heart and kidney disease, blindness, and amputation. While the numbers seem staggering, it's important to remember that type 2 diabetes is a lifestyle disease, meaning you can take steps now to avoid it or, if you already have it, control it.

Case in point: Walking for as little as 20 to 30 minutes a day can drastically reduce your risk. Even better: If you already have diabetes, exercise can offset your risk of complications and, in some cases, may reverse the disease completely. "Walking helps your body use excess sugar in your bloodstream for energy, which lowers your blood sugar," says Sheri Colberg-Ochs, PhD, a spokesperson for the American Diabetes Association and professor of exercise science at Old Dominion University.

While any activity—even a few laps around Target—helps, picking up the pace of your walk helps your body manage blood sugar more efficiently for anywhere from 2 to 72 hours.

Aim to chew your food thoroughly. Taste it. Enjoy it! Take a few extra minutes to pay attention to flavors and texture.

Put your fork down between bites. Chew and swallow before picking up your utensils again.

Talk to your dinner mates. It's not polite to talk with your mouth full, so focus on making conversation with family or friends to slow your pace.

Start a Movement

Research confirms what we've known all along: You'll walk more often if you bring a few friends. Here's how to organize the perfect peregrinating posse.

Recruit Right

To recruit group members, walking coach Michele Stanten recommends passing out flyers in your neighborhood, exercise classes, work, or at any clubs you're a part of. You can even check out websites such as ExcerciseFriends.com or walkers.meetup.com that allow you to search for walking buddies in your area. When considering potential members already in your social circles, think about the types of people you would enjoy spending time with. Aim for at least two other people committing before you get started, that way you still have a walking buddy if one can't show. Four or five members is a good number, but try to stay under 12—you don't want too many people walking in the streets, especially if it's a busier route.

Fix a Time . . .

. . . And make sure that time works for you. "If you're the leader, you can't be the one skipping out," Stanten says. If you have kids, try for a time right after school drop-off. If you work, try for an early morning meetup or during lunchtime. Just make sure your timing is consistent so the rest of the group can get into the routine and stick with it.

Pave a Smart Path

Make sure your meeting place is conveniently located. Translation: that 30-minute drive to the park is going to get really old really fast. If there aren't any parks nearby, walk right in your own neighborhood. Or, tie your walk to another weekly event. For instance, if you already meet your friends for coffee, start at the coffee shop and save coffee for after your walks. "Having it tie to something that you regularly do gives you that cue and makes you more likely to stick with it," Stanten says.

Keep It Together

Because everyone walks at different paces, it's natural that some group members will get ahead of the pack and others will fall behind. Once the power-walkers of the group have had some time to stride, Stanten recommends looping—or whistling for the power-walkers to come back—about halfway through the walk. That way the slower walkers won't feel as though they're holding back the group, and the faster walkers still log more steps with their quicker pace.

Make It Fun

"If you have a group that's interested in reading, you could always do a book club—read a book and then discuss it while you're walking," Stanten says. "If you have people who don't know each other, do little icebreakers as you're walking: Have people share stories and ask silly questions." It'll give everyone the chance to get to know each other and build new relationships—more reasons to keep on stepping.

3 Walking Games to Keep You Motivated

When it comes to exercise, it doesn't get any simpler than walking. The problem, of course, is that the same old neighborhood trek can get boring. Burn fat and keep it fun with these quirky walking workouts from fitness expert and certified strength and conditioning specialist Linda Melone.

The Game: Walk-and-Seek

- **THE RULES:** Pick a new route and walk until you find a coffee shop that you haven't tried before. Sip a cup before heading back at caffeinated speed.

- **THE WIN:** It's a great way to rack up mileage and keep your mind off the clock.

- **BEST FOR:** Urbanites and coffee addicts

The Game: Hill vs. You

- **THE RULES:** Find a hill that takes between 30 seconds and 2 minutes to climb. Set your timer and walk up the hill as fast as you can. Repeat 6 to 10 times, striving to shave off a few seconds with each climb to the top.

Yup, you are more brilliant after a walk! New research shows it can boost creative thinking by as much as 60 percent.

THE WIN: The rise in intensity will burn more calories, and the competition will keep you motivated to push harder until the very end.

BEST FOR: Anyone with access to an incline *(stairs work, too)*

The Game: Capture the Flower

THE RULES: Walk until you've taken snapshots of 10 beautiful landscapes. Post your favorites on Instagram, Twitter, or Facebook.

THE WIN: Endorphins + nature + "likes" on social media? It's the ultimate mood booster.

BEST FOR: Artistic souls, outdoor enthusiasts, and social media junkies

A Week of Walking

The Flat Belly Breakthrough program calls for a leisurely 30-minute walk after dinner. If you find yourself game for increasing your pace, try these options. Before starting any of the more intense walks described below, warm up and cool down by walking at an easy pace for 3 to 5 minutes.

	MONDAY	TUESDAY	WEDNESDAY	THURSDAY	FRIDAY	SATURDAY	SUNDAY
WALK SPEED	Brisk walk	Speed walk	Leisurely walk	Speed walk	Brisk walk	Speed walk	Leisurely walk

The Brisk Walk

This is a steady-paced, moderate-intensity walk, perfect for inviting a friend, family member, or coworker to join you (as long as that person doesn't hold you back). You should walk at a purposeful pace, as though hurrying to get to an appointment—about 3 to 4 mph. Do at least two brisk walks per week, aiming for a solid 30 minutes in weeks 1 to 4 and 30 to 40 minutes in weeks 5 to 12.

The Speed Walk

This walk adds fast-paced bouts. Do 3 speed walks (25 minutes each) per week in weeks 1 to 4 and two speed walks (25 to 30 minutes each) per week in weeks

5 to 12. Start with this interval: Walk for 4 minutes briskly, followed by 1 minute fast; repeat four times to complete the workout. Slowly progress until you're walking briskly for 1 minute, followed by 1 minute fast; repeat for your entire walk.

The Leisurely Walk

This is your regular slow to moderate walking pace. You can easily bring your dog along for company, or be able to hold a conversation with a friend without feeling winded. There's no specific mph to aim for, but your leisurely pace should last 30-35 minutes and cover about 1.5 miles.

Walk like a Pro

Want to up your speed and burn more calories? Fine-tune your form with these simple tips.

- Gaze 10 to 20 feet in front of you, not down at your feet.

- Keep your shoulders rolled back and down, not scrunched up by your ears.

- Bend your arms 90 degrees, keeping your hands in relaxed fists.

- Swing your arms forward and back (avoid side-to-side motion), squeezing your shoulder blades and driving your elbows behind you.

- Lean your torso forward slightly, about 5 degrees.

- Land on your heel as you swing your leg forward, squeezing through your glutes.

- Push off with your toes to propel yourself forward.

- Take short, quick steps. They allow for a smooth, rolling stride, which helps you walk faster.

Waterproof Your Walk

When conditions turn less than ideal, flip to this page for the seven best wet-weather secrets to see you cheerfully through the rain. Don't let showers (or snow) stop your program. (It's only water!)

- Wear garments that breathe. A plastic slicker may keep the rain out, but you'll get steamy on the inside.

- Stick to asphalt and concrete, but avoid the painted lines on roads; they can sometimes be slicker than the road surface. Keep off slippery wet grass, too.

- Choose leather walking shoes. They resist water better than cloth or nylon mesh. (Also, rippled soles give you better traction.)

- Wear bright clothing. You'll be more visible to drivers on rainy days.

- Use a hat or visor with a large brim to keep rain off your face. If you're still getting pelted, carry an umbrella: You can still get a brisk walk even if you aren't swinging your arms fully. And walking with an umbrella, no matter how it may slow you, is better than watching TV!

- Step around puddles. It may seem obvious, but for walkers who keep to a straight course, standing water may be deeper than it looks.

- Stuff your wet walking shoes with newspaper or paper towels to speed drying. SealSkinz socks are watertight, yet allow sweat to evaporate. Wear them with a pair of walking shoes, and you can splash around like Gene Kelly!

The Perfect Pair

Unless you're Carrie Bradshaw, you're probably not out walking in 4-inch Manolo Blahniks with barely a strap to keep them on. But you could be making a similar gaffe if you're taking your evening strolls in thin-soled tennis sneakers, high-tops, or athletic-looking footwear designed for fashion, not function. Wearing the wrong shoe—even a running shoe—can be a quick route back to the couch. Unfortunately, 72 percent of shoes bought for walking are not walking shoes, according to stats from the National Sporting Goods Association.

Walking shoes aren't just a marketing ploy. They're specifically designed for how we walk, which is very different from how we run. While runners land flat-footed, walkers land on their heels. So the heels of walking shoes are often slanted to increase stability. That stability is also important when you roll forward and push off with your toes, as you do when you walk. And you'll be less likely to trip because the soles of walking shoes are smoother than those of running shoes.

These walking-specific features can help keep you injury free, so it's worth the time to get the right shoe. Because no two pairs of feet are alike, we've included this guide to help you identify the kind of foot you have (there's more to it than size). There are three basic foot types—neutral, rigid, and flexible—that describe what your foot does every time you take a step. Shoes that best support your foot type will feel better and last longer because you'll put less stress on both foot and shoe. Here's how to determine your type.

The Wet Test

Dip your bare feet into a pan of water. Applying your full weight, step onto a piece of brown paper. Repeat until you get a crisp pattern of each foot. Before your prints fade, match them to those shown here. (If yours are somewhere between neutral and flexible, use neutral as your guide. If yours fall between neutral and rigid, choose rigid. If your footprints are different patterns, aim to fit the more flexible one.)

Neutral

You'll see about a 1-inch strip of wetness in the arch area.

How you tread: Your feet are well balanced and roll, or pronate, almost perfectly. Your feet lengthen and spread out about a half shoe size when you stand, and they absorb shock well and have good stability. But put these nearly perfect puppies in poorly fitted shoes, and you could be hobbled with blisters or other foot problems.

How to fit: Yours is the easiest foot to fit because many styles are designed for your type. Make sure any shoe you buy feels good in the store—no rubbing or pinching.

Rigid

Your arch is so high that you'll see little, if any, imprint in the arch area.

How you tread: Your feet tend to roll inward only slightly, so you underpronate, meaning you walk more on the outsides of your feet. They're stable, but they don't absorb shock well because they're stiff: They tend not to lengthen and spread out much when you stand.

How to fit: You need shoes that are well cushioned to absorb shock, and flexible enough to allow your feet to roll more. Go for a roomy upper to accommodate your high arch. Choose the shoe with the highest heel if you have tight calves, which is common in this foot type. Your feet are also likely to curve inward at the ball (you can check this out by tracing your feet), so look for a shoe that does likewise by matching the tracings of your feet to the soles of shoes you're considering.

Flexible

Your foot is flat and has a low arch. It will leave the fullest imprint, with the most arch area in contact with the paper.

How you tread: Your feet roll inward too much (overpronate) when you walk. They're unstable, but they absorb shock well because they spread out: They change an entire size when you stand.

How to fit: Because your feet tend to flatten, you need a shoe that has less space between the laces and the sole. (To judge height, move your feet up and down inside the front of the shoes while you're wearing them.) You don't need a lot of cushioning, but you do need good arch support so your feet don't completely flatten when you step. Also, a lower-heeled shoe, as compared with other shoes, will help keep your feet more stable while you walk.

Your 10 Biggest Walking Pains, Solved

We all know that walking is the safest, easiest form of exercise, so why should you bother reading up on the risks? Because, left ignored, an innocent foot pain or leg pain can become a chronic problem. Each year, nearly 250,000 walkers are hobbled as a result of a walking-induced pain or a nagging old exercise injury that walking has aggravated. As bothersome as the initial problem can be, the real damage is what happens next. You stop exercising, misplace your motivation, and soon gain weight and lose muscle tone. To make sure a debilitating walking injury doesn't prevent you from reaching your fitness and weight-loss goals, we asked leading experts for advice on how to avoid aches and treat the 10 most common walking pains.

Plantar Fasciitis

Feels like: Tenderness on your heel or bottom of foot

What it is: The plantar fascia is the band of tissue that runs from your heel bone to the ball of your foot. When this dual-purpose shock absorber and arch support is strained, small tears develop and the tissue stiffens as a protective response, causing foot pain. "Walkers can overwork the area when pounding the pavement, especially when you wear hard shoes on concrete, because there's very little give as the foot lands," says Teresa Schuemann, a physical therapist in Fort Collins, Colorado, and a spokesperson for the American Physical Therapy Association. You know you have plantar fasciitis if you feel pain in your heel or arch first thing in the morning, because the fascia stiffens during the night.

What to do about it: At the first sign of stiffness in the bottom of your foot, loosen up the tissue by doing this stretch: Sit with ankle of injured foot across opposite thigh. Pull toes toward shin with hand until you feel a stretch in arch. Run your opposite hand along sole of foot; you should feel a taut band of tissue. Do 10 stretches, holding each for 10 seconds. Then stand and massage your foot by rolling it on a golf ball or full water bottle.

To reduce pain, wear supportive shoes or sandals with a contoured footbed at all times. Choose walking shoes that are not too flexible in the middle. See the guide on page 197, or seek off-the-shelf orthotic inserts (by Dr. Scholl's or Vionic, for example. Until you can walk pain free, stick to flat, stable, giving paths (such as a level dirt road) and avoid pavement, sand, and uneven ground that might cause too much flexing at the arch, says Phillip Ward, DPM, a podiatrist in Pinehurst, North Carolina.

Ingrown Toenail

Feels like: Soreness or swelling on the sides of your toes

What it is: Toe pain can develop when the corners or sides of your toenails grow sideways rather than forward, putting pressure on surrounding soft tissues and even growing into the skin. You may be more likely to develop ingrown toenails if your shoes are too short or too tight, which causes repeated trauma to the toe as you walk.

What to do about it: Leave wiggle room in your shoes. You may need to go up a half size when you buy sneakers, because your feet tend to swell during exercise. Use toenail clippers (not fingernail clippers or scissors) to cut straight across instead of rounding the corners when you give yourself a pedicure. If you have diabetes or any circulatory disorder, have your ingrown toenails treated by a podiatrist.

Bunion

Feels like: Pain on the side of your big toe

What it is: A bunion develops when the bones in the joint on the outer side of the big or little toe become misaligned, forming a painful swelling. Walkers with flat feet, low arches, or arthritis may be more apt to develop bunions.

What to do about it: "Wear shoes that are wider—especially in the toe box," says Dr. Ward. If you don't want to shell out for new shoes, ask your shoe repair guy to stretch the old ones. Cushioning the bunion with OTC pads can provide relief, and icing it for 20 minutes after walking will numb the area.

Achilles Tendinitis

Feels like: Pain in the back of your heel and lower calf

What it is: The Achilles tendon, which connects your calf muscle to your heel, can be irritated by walking too much, especially if you don't build up to it. Repeated flexing of the foot when walking up and down steep hills or on uneven terrain can also strain the tendon, triggering lower leg pain.

What to do about it: For mild cases, reduce your mileage or substitute non-weight-bearing activities such as swimming or upper-body strength training, so long as these don't aggravate the pain. "Avoid walking uphill, because this increases the stretch on the tendon, irritating it and making it weaker," says Dr. Schuemann. Regular calf stretches may help prevent Achilles tendinitis. In severe cases, limit or stop walking and place cold packs on the injured area for 15 to 20 minutes, up to four times a day, to reduce inflammation and pain. When you return to walking, stick to flat surfaces to keep your foot in a neutral position, and gradually increase your distance and intensity.

Lumbar Strain

Feels like: Ache in your mid to lower back

What it is: Walking doesn't usually cause lower-back pain, but the repetitive movement can make an existing lower-back injury worse. It's easy to "throw out your back" when tendons and ligaments around the spine are overworked. Arthritis or inflammation of surrounding nerves can also cause pain in this region.

What to do about it: For general back pain prevention, keep the muscles in your trunk strong. While you walk, engage your abs by pulling your belly button toward your spine as if you were trying to flatten your belly to zip up tight jeans.

A short pull exercise might also prevent slumping by realigning your posture. You can even do it while you walk! Simply cross your arms at wrists in front of your waist and raise arms as if you're pulling a shirt up over your head. Grow taller as you reach up, then lower your arms, letting your shoulders drop into place.

Neuroma

Feels like: Pain in the ball of your foot or between toes

What it is: If tissue surrounding a nerve near the base of the toes thickens, it can cause tingling, numbness, or pain that radiates to surrounding areas. It may feel as though you're treading on a marble. This condition, known as Morton's neuroma, frequently develops between the base of the third and fourth toes. It's up to 10 times more common in women than men, possibly because women's feet are structured differently and because we tend to wear narrow, high shoes or very flat ones.

What to do about it: Treatment varies from simply wearing roomier shoes to surgery, depending upon the severity of the neuroma. See a podiatrist at the first sign of foot pain, as this condition can worsen quickly. Make sure that your walking shoes have a spacious toe box. Limit your time spent hoofing it in heels, and, if you must wear them, travel in comfy shoes such as supportive ballet flats and then slip on the more stylish pair.

Shin Splints

Feels like: Stiffness or soreness in your shins

What it is: Your shins have to bear up to six times your weight while you exercise, so foot-pounding activities such as walking and running can cause problems for the muscles and surrounding tissues and create inflammation. The strain and leg pain results from strong calves pulling repeatedly on weaker muscles near the shin. Spending too many hours walking on concrete can also lead to this sort of inflammation. Severe or pinpointed pain in the shin could also be a stress fracture of the tibia.

What to do about it: Keep your walks at a leisurely, low-impact stroll, or try cross-training with low-impact exercises such as swimming or cycling. You should strengthen the muscles in the front of the lower leg (anterior tibialis) to help prevent a recurrence.

Use this simple exercise: While standing, lift toes toward shins 20 times. Work up to 3 sets and, as you get stronger, lay a 2- or 3-pound ankle weight across your toes to add more resistance. Once you're ready to start walking again, choose a dirt path and walk for 20 minutes at a moderate pace. Increase distance or speed slightly each week. "If your shins start to feel sore, rest for a day or two, and when you exercise again, take it even more slowly," says Byron Russell, PhD, chair of the department of physical therapy at Eastern Washington University.

Bursitis

Feels like: Soreness on the outside of your hips

What it is: Although there are many potential causes of hip pain, it's common for the fluid-filled sacs (bursae) that cushion the hip joint to become inflamed with repetitive stress. People with one leg slightly longer than the other are more susceptible to this kind of hip pain. Too much walking without building up to it can also be a cause.

What to do about it: Instead of walking, ride a stationary bike, swim, or do some other non-weight-bearing activity for a few weeks. When you begin walking again, don't just step back in where you left off. Start gradually: Walk every other day at first. Spend the first 5 minutes warming up by walking slowly, and do the last 5 minutes at a slower, cool-down pace.

Runner's Knee

Feels like: Throbbing in front of your kneecap

What it is: Every time your shoe strikes the ground, your knee feels it. Walkers with a misaligned kneecap, prior injury, weak or imbalanced thigh muscles, soft knee cartilage, or flat feet, or those who simply walk too much, are at greater risk of runner's knee. The knee pain usually strikes when you're walking downhill, doing knee bends, or sitting for a long stretch of time.

What to do about it: Shift to another type of exercise until the knee pain subsides, typically 8 to 12 weeks. Do some quad strengtheners to help align the kneecap and beef up support around your knee: Sit with your back against a wall, right leg bent with foot flat on floor and left leg straight in front of you. Contract quads and lift left leg, keeping foot flexed. Repeat 12 times; work up to 3 sets per leg. While standing, place a looped band around both feet and sidestep 12 to 15 times to right, then back to left. When walking downhill, take smaller steps and try not to bend your knees too much, or try walking sideways to give your side hip muscles a workout.

Stress Fracture

Feels like: Acute pain in your foot or lower leg

What it is: If you feel tenderness or pain when you press on a specific spot on your foot or lower leg, you may have a stress fracture—a tiny crack in a bone. Most common in the lower leg, stress fractures tend to occur when your leg muscles become overloaded from repetitive stress because the shock is absorbed by the bone, rather than the muscle. This can happen if you ignore a shin splint, for instance, because the continued strain on muscles and tissues will eventually shift to the bone. Walking is more likely to lead to a stress fracture if you walk for too long without building up to it, especially if you have high arches or rigid, flat feet. Women may be more vulnerable because their lower muscle mass and bone density don't always act as adequate shock absorbers.

What to do about it: Kick back and let your foot or leg pain heal for several weeks. "You need to get off your feet to avoid loading the bones," says Sheila Dugan, MD, a physiatrist and an associate professor at Rush Medical College. Replace walking with swimming, water aerobics, or upper-body weight training. When you return to your regular regimen, stop before you feel any discomfort. "If you walk 1 mile and experience symptoms again, slow down and start walking a quarter mile and take several weeks to build up to the longer distance," says Russell. Replace walking shoes when the interior cushioning has worn down, to ensure that you have adequate shock absorption. To optimize bone health, do lower-body strength-training twice a week and eat calcium-rich food such as yogurt and cheese and greens such as kale, or take a supplement. You need 1,000 mg of calcium a day (1,200 mg if you're 51 or older).

The Truth about Stretching

Think about the last powerful rainstorm you experienced and how the fierce winds bent the tree branches nearly to the ground. After the storm, what became of those trees?

If the trees were big, old, and brittle, it's likely that pieces of their mighty branches lay strewn over the ground while the saplings and young, more supple trees in your yard bounced back and remained standing after the winds died down.

With age and inactivity, our own limbs can become stiff and rigid like an old oak tree. And our bodies can't bounce back after being stressed the way they did in our sapling years. But that's not the only downside: A stiff, inflexible body takes more effort to move, which discourages movement. And if you hesitate to move in order to avoid soreness or pain, you become less active and burn fewer calories. As a result, you add pounds, which can further hamper your flexibility and movement. It's a spiral of inactivity, pain, and weight gain.

The goal of this section is to help you to increase your flexibility, avoid injury, and build resilience to take full advantage of the belly-shrinking benefits of the Flat Belly Breakthrough program.

Better Posture, Flatter Belly

You don't even have to try touching your toes to know if you could benefit from greater flexibility. Just check out your posture in a full-length mirror, while wearing a swimsuit, or have a friend take photos of you from the front and side. Are your shoulders and back rounded? Does your belly push forward? Does your head protrude outward? All of these are signs of poor posture, weak muscles, and inflexibility, a cascade of structural flaws that can result in stiffness, joint pain, and weak muscles, all of which can compromise your ability to burn fat.

Try this: While looking at yourself sideways in a bathroom mirror, force yourself to stand upright with good posture, chest out, and shoulders back. What happens to the look of your belly? It should automatically retract, making you look instantly thinner even if you didn't follow my diet and exercise program. Do you see the power of greater flexibility and a straight-arrow posture?

What Determines Flexibility

Flexibility is defined as the range of movement of a body segment around a joint or group of joints. Young children are normally very flexible, but as they grow older they lose some of their range of movement. This is partially unavoidable, as some of a child's flexibility results from the fact that the bones are soft and the limbs are fairly thin. Both change with age. But a certain part of the flexibility loss that occurs between childhood and maturity is the direct result of failing to stretch.

You can maintain a fairly normal range of movement without much in the way of stretching, just as you can keep a moderate level of strength without doing progressive resistance exercise. But without a systematic program of strength training, which involves both contraction and stretching of the major muscles, you will gradually lose both strength and flexibility as you age. There's no doubt about it.

Have you ever seen elderly men and women who seem barely able to lift their feet as they shuffle across the floor? Have you seen an old person who had difficulty rising out of a chair? Both are the result of lack of muscular strength and flexibility. The bottom line: Even if you are many decades away from being considered elderly, you need strength and flexibility now to perform effectively in daily living. That doesn't mean you need to be as flexible as a gymnast or dancer. Not everyone has the ability to be that limber. Several factors influence how much flexibility you can develop. Let's examine them:

Anatomical: Tendons, ligaments, muscle fascia, and muscle fibers react differently to stretching. Tendons, the strong fibers that attach muscles to bones, are not meant to be stretched. Ligaments are fibers that link bones to other bones. They adapt to slight stretching, but once stretched will not return to normal length. The muscle fascia, an elastic connective tissue sheath enclosing muscle fibers, can stretch and become more flexible. The muscle fibers themselves probably have the most potential for stretching. An individual's absolute maximum range of movement is determined genetically. Some people simply have a greater capacity for flexibility than others.

Neurological: Nerve receptors in the muscles, tendons, and ligaments are sensitive to tension. When a muscle is stretched suddenly, its stretch reflex automatically responds with a contraction that varies with the suddenness and intensity of the stretch. You've experienced this anytime you fall asleep while seated in a chair and your head nods forward and causes the next extensor muscles to suddenly stretch. The stretch reflex responds by jerking your head back into the erect position. The stretch reflex also helps you jump when you dip down and load your leg muscles prior to a jump. Another example is when a baseball player cocks his bat backward before swinging at the ball.

Age and inactivity: Flexibility decreases with age or inactivity. Muscle fascia and ligaments are particularly susceptible to tightening. Have you ever had your arm or leg in a cast? When the cast comes off, your limb is ridged and lacks range of motion. Lack of exercise gradually produces the same result.

Unbalanced muscular development: Runners often have very tight hamstrings because their training creates a strength imbalance in their legs. Poor posture or walking habits can also cause unbalanced muscle development, which can affect flexibility.

Temperature: Research shows that warming an area of the body increases the involved muscles' flexibility by as much as 20 percent. Cooling a body part decreases it 10 to 20 percent. This is why you should always warm your body before stretching your muscles. You can do this simply by marching in place, jumping rope, swinging your arms, or doing jumping jacks.

Stretching: The Key to Flexibility

The critical word in increasing flexibility is *stretching.* Stretching occurs when a movement exceeds an existing range of movement. But you cannot simply move into a stretched position. Instead, you must be forced into a stretch by a resistance that pushes or pulls your body part into that position. The resistance may be provided by an exercise machine, such as the Nautilus, by certain barbell and dumbbell exercises, or your body weight or muscular force.

The following freehand-yoga-type movements are ideal stretches for beginners. Perform them several times a week. You can do them in the morning, in the evening after your 30-minute after dinner walk, or after your regular workouts. Hold each stretch for 10 to 15 seconds and repeat once after a 5-second rest. And make sure you always warm up before stretching.

Sitting Thigh Stretch

Muscles worked: Hamstrings

Starting position: Sit on floor with the legs extended.

Movement: Bend forward from the waist and try to reach beyond the toes. Grasp the feet or ankles and pull with the arms to force the hamstrings into a slow stretch.

Kneeling Thigh Stretch

Muscles worked: Quadriceps

Starting position: Kneel with your toes extended. Keep your trunk in line with your thighs.

Movement: Bend smoothly backwards at the knees. Use your hands for support.

Groin Stretch

Muscles worked: Adductor group

Starting position: In a seated position, spread your knees and put the soles of your feet together. Your elbows should be placed on the inside of your knees.

Movement: Press gently the inside of your knees with your elbows.

Upper Back Stretch

Muscles worked: Deltoid (shoulders) and erector spinae group, or the muscles running on either side of your spine from your neck to your pelvis

Starting position: Lie flat on your back with palms down and by your sides.

Movement: Raise your legs up and over your head. Keep your arms and hands on the floor as a stretch is felt in your upper back.

Lower Trunk Stretch

Muscles worked: Abdominals and inner hip muscles

Starting position: Lie on your stomach, bend your knees, and grasp your ankles from behind.

Movement: Pull slowly with arms and hold.

Twisting Trunk Stretch

Muscles worked: Gluteus medius (butt muscles), erector spinae group, and obliques

Starting position: Sit in a cross-legged position with your right leg over your left. Your right ankle should be near your right knee. Twist your trunk to the right and place your left arm on the side of your right leg.

Movement: Keep your trunk twisted and push against your right leg with your left arm. Stretch and hold. Reverse your position and repeat to the other side.

Forward Bend in Chair

Muscles worked: Erector spinae group

Starting position: Sit in a chair with your hips well back and your feet about 24 inches apart.

Movement: Bend forward from the waist. Your upper body should pass between your knees. Reach under the chair bottom as far as possible. Stretch and hold.

Shoulder Circles

Muscles worked: Deltoid and chest major

Starting position: Grasp a rope, belt, or towel with your hands approximately 3 feet apart. Keep your arms straight throughout.

Movement: Move the tightly stretched rope slowly over your head and behind your back. Stretch and return to the starting position. To make the movement harder, move your hands closer together.

Onward

We've hit on a lot of important concepts: journaling, meal planning, substitute meals, grocery shopping, measurements, before-and-after photos, body-fat determination, exercise charting, record keeping, water drinking, sleeping and resting, motivation, walking, injury prevention, and stretching.

The discipline and patience of it all is now up to you. But you are well prepared with plenty of ammunition for a successful journey.

I want to hear from you. I look forward to seeing and hearing about your leaner, stronger belly, butt, and thighs.

Yes, your brand-new body will soon be a reality. Work hard and stay in touch.

—Ellington Darden, PhD
Visit him at www.DrDarden.com